BEYOND THE VEIL: EMPOWERING TRANSFORMATION IN THE DISSOCIATED MIND

A COMPASSIONATE GUIDE TO DISSOCIATIVE DISORDERS, TRAUMA RECOVERY, AND PERSONAL EMPOWERMENT WITH PRACTICAL COPING SKILLS AND ENGAGING WORKSHEETS

KENNEDY ALLEN

CONTENTS

PART ONE
DISSECTING DISSOCIATION

PART TWO
OVERCOMING WITH SELF-HELP STRATEGIES

INTRODUCTION

In the human mind, there exists a balance between thoughts, feelings, and memories, yet for some of us, this delicate balance fractures into a maze of disconnection. This is generally due to dissociative disorders, which cast shadows on our minds. These disorders affect an estimated 1% to 5% of the global population. Among them, dissociative identity disorder (DID), formerly known as multiple personality disorder, stands as a rare and enigmatic presence that touches the lives of approximately 1.5% of the world's population (Ferguson, 2023).

In this state of dissociation, our thoughts, memories, and emotions become elusive ghosts that constantly slip away from our grasp, much like sand slipping through our fingers. We tend to feel as if we have two or more entities within us, each with its own way of thinking and remembering about ourselves and our lives. This is our reality. We not only face internal struggles but also encounter external challenges that manifest in our daily lives.

The extent of our challenges varies widely. First, we tend to find ourselves on a solitary journey, navigating through the dense fog of social isolation and stigmatization. Our conditions, often misunderstood, cast a heavy weight upon us, which leads to feelings of loneliness, shame, and rejection. This isolation becomes a breeding ground for our mental health difficulties, which turns our daily existence into a battleground where our very sense of self is relentlessly under siege.

Also, the pages of our life stories are stained with the indelible ink of unresolved trauma. This ink contributes to the manifestation of dissociative symptoms that lead to emotional pain, flashbacks, and nightmares in our lives. These relentless adversaries create a constant struggle, a battle waged against our memories echoing through the corridors of our minds, which impacts our ability to function in the present.

Amidst this tumult, a pervasive sense of confusion and emotional distress lingers, stemming from our struggles to understand and articulate our dissociative experiences. The lack of comprehension surrounding our mental health challenges leaves us feeling adrift in a sea of incomprehensibility, as if our internal struggles are lost in translation.

Moreover, dissociation, with its interference in our daily lives, forces us onto a precarious tightrope walk. Our work, relationships, and overall well-being hang in the balance, teetering on the edge as the weight of responsibilities becomes a Herculean task. Frustration, self-doubt, and a sense of helplessness become our constant companions in the struggle to maintain balance.

The thick shroud of stigma surrounding our mental health further complicates our lives, which makes it challenging to seek professional help. This reluctance, in turn, leads to delayed intervention, which exacerbates our symptoms and nurtures a haunting sense of hopelessness in our quest for effective support.

The collateral damage to strained relationships is an additional burden, as we tend to struggle with the unpredictable nature of dissociative episodes. The aftermath includes feelings of guilt, a fear of rejection, and the painful loss of meaningful connections with friends, family, or partners. In our struggles, ineffective coping strategies often compound our pain. In the end, we may resort to harmful mechanisms, perpetuating negative cycles that push us further away from the elusive path to healing.

Also, identity and self-concept become key challenges, especially when you are struggling with DID. This condition fosters a fragmented sense of self, giving rise to internal conflicts and multiple identities that leave you feeling untethered in a vast sea of uncertainty regarding your own identity. The multiple identities differ in your perceptions, memories, and characteristics, which contributes to a disjointed and elusive understanding of your core self. This internal discord can lead to a significant struggle in trying to integrate and reconcile these contradictory aspects, making the process of developing a stable and cohesive sense of identity very difficult.

Lastly, a perpetual shadow of fear of the unknown looms large over our lives. The unpredictable nature of dissociative experiences begets anxiety, constant apprehension, hypervigilance, and a fundamental difficulty in trusting ourselves. The overwhelming emotions triggered by past trauma or dissociative experiences prove insurmountable and challenging to manage, casting pervasive darkness over our daily existence.

Despite all of these challenges, we often long for understanding, validation, and healing. Now, you may ask yourself, "How would I go about a life where the very essence of my thoughts and emotions remains just unreachable, like trying to catch a fleeting breeze?" Well, it is at this particular moment that this book comes into play. It comes as a beacon of hope that provides both realistic and compassionate ways to go through this maze of dissociation. It offers methods for overcoming each of these difficulties, stressing the need for not simply surviving the storm, but also growing from it. With the help of this book, empowerment—a lighthouse that shines in the dark and offers coping mechanisms for healing and recuperation—becomes your ally that propels you towards a future free from the constraints of dissociation. Also, this book offers practical shortcuts to self-awareness, improved relationships, and enhanced functioning. Just keep in mind that it's a companion on your path to a better and more rewarding future—not just a guidebook.

This book promises a life where the shadows of dissociation recede and are eventually replaced by the warm embrace of self-awareness and acceptance. Relationships, once strained, are mended. Daily functioning is no longer a battleground but a center for meaningful experiences. The fear of the unknown dissipates, which gives way to a life that is characterized by confidence, trust, and tranquility. You will be equipped with a strong understanding of dissociative disorders, empowered by practical tools and strategies. You'll confidently navigate daily challenges, foster supportive relationships, and start a journey that will ultimately lead to healing, resilience, and a restored sense of control over your mental health.

As your guide through this journey, I provide not only knowledge but also a deep understanding derived from both personal and professional experience. I have made my way through this maze, discovered the keys to recovery, and am now ready to share these insights with you. I, too, once struggled with the challenges of dissociation, traversing a path full of uncertainty. Because of the obstacles I overcame, I am in a unique position to help you navigate this dark point in life. Believe me when I say that walking through this path is not a simple task, but with proper guidance, you can actually be empowered to discover the strength within yourself, find clarity amid the confusion, and emerge into the light of healing and understanding.

So, in the warmth of these pages, you will find not just words but a lifeline to understanding, healing, and transformation. This book speaks to the very heart of your struggles, offering solace, guidance, and the promise of a brighter tomorrow.

PART ONE
DISSECTING DISSOCIATION

CHAPTER 1
UNDERSTANDING DISSOCIATIVE DISORDERS

Dissociative disorders are like a fragmented puzzle, each piece representing a distinct facet of one's identity. In the chaotic jumble, some pieces fade away, lost to the depths of the mind. The puzzle, once interconnected, forms a composition of experiences, memories, and emotions.

DISSOCIATIVE DISORDERS

Before going any deeper, let's first understand: What exactly is dissociation? It is a mental process in which a person's thoughts, feelings, sensations, or memories become disconnected from one another. It is a coping mechanism that the mind uses to manage overwhelming stress or trauma. During dissociation, you may feel detached from yourself or your surroundings, as if you are watching events unfold from a distance.

Consequently, dissociative disorders emerge as mental conditions involving disconnections in thoughts, memories, feelings, surroundings, behavior, and identity, resulting in an unhealthy escape from reality. This disconnection poses challenges in managing daily life. Some dissociative disorders are transient, resolving in weeks or months, often linked to traumatic events, while others persist over an extended period, presenting a more enduring challenge. While not officially diagnosed, many people report experiencing dissociative symptoms. These disorders are trickier to diagnose as compared to bipolar disorder or major depressive disorder (MDD).

Symptoms of a Dissociative Disorder

The following symptoms collectively portray the complex and often challenging nature of dissociative disorders, involving disruptions in perception, identity, memory, and overall mental well-being.

- **Anxiety:** You may find yourself experiencing a heightened sense of worry, fear, or unease, and these feelings could become intense and overwhelming.
- **Delusions:** You might find that you hold false beliefs or perceptions that are not grounded in reality, which often involve misinterpretations of events or situations.
- **Depression:** At certain points, you might experience a continuous and widespread feeling of unhappiness, despair, and a diminished enthusiasm or enjoyment in activities that once brought you happiness.
- **Disorientation:** You could experience moments of confusion or a sense of being lost in terms of time, place, or even your personal identity.
- **Memory loss:** You may encounter gaps in your memory, which range from forgetting specific events or time periods to more extensive amnesia. You might lose awareness or memory of specific periods, events, or personal details, which can be distressing and disorienting.

- **Substance use disorder:** You might engage in problematic and potentially harmful patterns of substance use, such as drugs or alcohol, as a way to cope with emotional distress.
- **Suicidal thoughts or self-harm:** There might be times when you contemplate or engage in thoughts of self-harm or suicide, reflecting significant emotional distress.
- **Feeling disconnected from yourself and the world around you:** You could experience a sense of detachment or unreality, as if you are observing your life from a distance rather than actively participating.
- **Feeling uncertain about who you are:** You may experience a lack of a stable sense of self or identity, contributing to feelings of confusion and insecurity about your own identity.
- **Having multiple distinct identities:** There could be instances when you perceive the presence of different personalities or identities within yourself, often associated with dissociative identity disorder.
- **Feeling little or no physical pain:** You might experience reduced sensitivity to physical pain, which can be a manifestation of dissociation from your own body.

TYPES OF DISSOCIATIVE DISORDERS

There are several types of dissociative disorders, each characterized by disruptions in memory, identity, consciousness, or perception. The main types include:

Dissociative Identity Disorder (DID)

DID is a complex and rare mental health condition that is characterized by the presence of two or more distinct identities or personality states within an individual. Each identity, commonly referred to as an "alter," possesses its own way of perceiving and interacting with the world. These alters may have distinct names, personal histories, and even physical characteristics.

Then, switching is the phenomenon that is central to DID and involves a rapid transition between different alters. Switching can be triggered by stress, trauma, or other internal or external stimuli. During a switch, your behavior, voice, mannerisms, and even physiological responses may change as you transition from one alter to another. This process of switching can be abrupt and may occur without your conscious awareness.

Alters in DID are unique coping mechanisms that are developed in response to traumatic experiences, especially those occurring in childhood. They often emerge to shield you from overwhelming emotions, memories, or situations that would otherwise be too distressing to handle. The presence of alters allows you to compartmentalize your experiences, with each alter carrying a specific role or function within the system.

Communication between alters can vary widely. Some individuals with DID may experience amnesia between switches, which means that one alter may not have awareness of the actions or experiences of another alter. In contrast, co-consciousness refers to a state where two or more alters are aware of each other's existence and activities. The level of co-consciousness can fluctuate, influencing the person's overall sense of self-awareness.

To understand how alters work, consider the story of Emma. She has struggled with DID from the age of 12. Her days were full of navigating the distinct identities that coexisted within her. Each morning, she would wake up uncertain of which identity would take the lead.

Emma's day began with the gentle and nurturing presence of Lily, her primary alter. Lily would meticulously plan the day, leaving notes for Emma to follow. Emma's coworkers knew Lily as the responsible and organized team player who effortlessly managed the demands of her job at the local library. Lily was the one who handled meetings, interacted with colleagues, and maintained a veneer of normalcy.

As the day unfolded, Lily's presence would gradually recede, making way for a more carefree and adventurous alter named Max. Max loved exploring the world and trying new things. During Max's time, Emma might impulsively decide to take a spontaneous road trip or immerse herself in painting, Max's favorite hobby. Max's zest for life brought a burst of energy and creativity to Emma's routine.

However, not all alters were as benign. In the evening, a solemn and introspective alter named Olivia emerged. Olivia held the memories of trauma that led to the development of DID. Her presence brought a heaviness to Emma, and during this time, she preferred solitude, often retreating into the solace of her favorite books.

Navigating social relationships was a challenge. Emma's friends had to learn to recognize the subtle shifts in her behavior, adapting to the different alters as they emerged. Lily, Max, and Olivia coexisted in a delicate balance, each contributing to Emma's multifaceted identity.

At night, Emma found solace in her therapist's office, where she worked diligently to integrate the distinct identities. Through therapy, she gained tools to communicate with her alters and foster a sense of cohesion. Emma's journey with DID was one of resilience, self-discovery, and the gradual integration of her fragmented self into a pattern of healing and understanding.

Dissociative Amnesia

Dissociative amnesia involves the mind selectively blocking significant aspects of personal information, creating memory gaps. Unlike ordinary forgetfulness, this protective mechanism shields individuals from distressing or traumatic experiences. Although the memories remain intact, access to them is restricted. Often triggered by severe trauma such as abuse, war, or natural disasters, dissociative amnesia poses a high risk of self-harm or suicidal behaviors. This condition emphasizes the relationship between memory, trauma, and mental well-being, emphasizing the need for understanding and support in addressing the challenges it presents. The following are the four types of dissociative amnesia:

- **Localized amnesia:**

Localizing itself within specific, often traumatic, time frames, localized amnesia serves as a protective mechanism, sheltering the mind from overwhelming experiences. Individuals with localized amnesia might exhibit a profound lack of recall for a particular period, blocking out events that pose a threat to their emotional well-being. For instance, a person might be unable to remember the details of a car accident, an assault, or another distressing incident that occurred during a defined time frame. The memory void acts as a psychological safeguard, preserving the individual's emotional equilibrium.

- **Selective amnesia:**

Selective amnesia delicately curates memory, which allows for the retention of some details while obscuring others. In this nuanced form of dissociative amnesia, individuals may recall specific events or aspects of their lives while remaining oblivious to others. For example, someone might vividly remember their childhood home but draw a blank when asked about significant family events during that time. The mind becomes a curator, selectively preserving fragments of the past, shielding the individual from the full weight of their experiences.

- **Generalized amnesia:**

Generalized amnesia casts a wide net, shrouding an individual's entire life history in a blanket of forgetfulness. Unlike the localized or selective variants, generalized amnesia erases memories across various domains, which leaves a person with a pervasive sense of memory loss. Imagine waking up one day and finding that everything in your life has been wiped clean—a sense of self, relationships, and experiences all veiled in a fog of forgetfulness. This kind of amnesia often arises as a response to severe trauma, and the individual may struggle to recall not only specific events but also fundamental aspects of their identity.

- **Systematized amnesia:**

Systematized amnesia introduces a degree of organization to the chaotic landscape of forgotten memories. In this form, individuals experience memory loss in a systematic, thematic manner. For instance, someone may selectively forget memories related to a specific person, place, or topic. This organized retreat of memories may serve as a defense mechanism against specific triggers, allowing the individual to navigate life while sidestepping the emotional landmines associated with the forgotten elements.

To illustrate what dissociative amnesia looks like, let's look at this story about Sarah. Sarah sat alone in her dimly lit apartment, staring blankly at the walls. She couldn't shake off the overwhelming sense of confusion and unease that had consumed her for days. As she attempted to recall the events leading up to this moment, her mind felt like a foggy maze with no clear pathways.

A few weeks before that, Sarah had been a successful marketing executive, managing multiple projects with ease. But now, it was as if a thick curtain had fallen, blocking her memories. She couldn't remember the specifics of her last client meeting, or even what she had for breakfast that morning.

One day, while browsing through old photos on her phone, Sarah stumbled upon images of a tropical vacation she couldn't recognize. As she swiped through the pictures, a wave of disorientation washed over her. She couldn't recall a single detail about the trip or the people she appeared to be vacationing with.

Concerned, Sarah decided to seek help from a therapist, hoping to unravel the mystery of her forgotten experiences. In the therapy session, she struggled to articulate her feelings and experiences, as if the memories were just beyond her grasp. The therapist, recognizing the symptoms, diagnosed Sarah with dissociative amnesia—a condition where traumatic or distressing events lead to significant memory loss as a coping mechanism.

Depersonalization-Derealization Disorder

Depersonalization-derealization disorder is a mental health condition characterized by persistent feelings of detachment from oneself (depersonalization) and a sense of unreality or disconnection from the external world (derealization). The condition can cause a person to feel as though they are an outsider witnessing their own life, which can cause a severe emotional numbness. These encounters might be upsetting and make it difficult to go about your everyday business. Although the exact reasons are unknown, trauma or extreme stress may be contributing factors.

Meet Alex, a 28-year-old graphic designer who, unbeknownst to him, was grappling with depersonalization-derealization disorder. His journey into this surreal realm began gradually, like a subtle fog creeping into his reality. Initially, Alex found himself detached from his own body, as if observing himself from a distance. He described it as an unsettling sensation, akin to living in a dream that refused to dissipate upon waking.

One day, while working on a tight deadline, Alex experienced a sudden surge of derealization. The vibrant colors of his design software became muted, and the edges of objects blurred into a disorienting haze. His once familiar studio now felt alien, as if he had been transported to a parallel dimension. The walls seemed to breathe, pulsating with an eerie rhythm that intensified his sense of unreality.

As the weeks passed, depersonalization intensified its grip. Alex struggled to recognize his own reflection in the mirror, his face morphing into an unfamiliar mask. Conversations with friends felt like distant echoes, and emotions became elusive specters, hovering just out of reach. He became a mere spectator in the theater of his life, detached from the emotional nuances that once defined him.

The disorder reached its zenith during a routine commute. In the midst of a crowded subway, Alex felt like a ghost navigating through a sea of phantoms. Faces blurred into featureless silhouettes, and the cacophony of the city became a muffled symphony. Overwhelmed by the disconnect between his inner self and the external world, Alex retreated further into the recesses of his mind.

Other Specified Dissociative Disorders (OSDD)

This is a category in the Diagnostic and Statistical Manual of Mental Disorders (DSM-5) that includes various dissociative disorders that do not fit the criteria for specific diagnoses. Here are a few examples:

- **Dissociative amnesia with dissociative fugue:**

In this subtype of OSDD, individuals experience memory loss along with a sudden and unexpected journey away from their home or usual surroundings. During this fugue state, they may assume a new identity and may not recall their past or how they ended up in a different location.

- **Depersonalization/derealization disorder not otherwise specified (NOS):**

This category may include individuals who experience symptoms of depersonalization or derealization that do not meet the full criteria for a specific diagnosis. It could involve atypical sensations of unreality, detachment, or distorted perceptions of the self and the environment.

- **Identity disturbance due to prolonged and intense stress:**

Some individuals may develop dissociative symptoms, such as identity disturbance, as a response to prolonged and intense stress. This could manifest as significant changes in self-perception, memory gaps, or a blurred sense of identity without meeting the criteria for a specific dissociative disorder.

- **Dissociative trance disorder:**

This involves episodes of trance or possession-like states that are not related to a recognized cultural or religious practice. During these episodes, individuals may appear to be in a different state of consciousness, and their behavior may be influenced by this altered state.

- **Recurrent absorption episodes:**

Individuals experiencing recurrent absorption episodes may frequently become intensely absorbed in their thoughts, fantasies, or daydreams, to the extent that they temporarily lose awareness of their surroundings. These absorption episodes can significantly impact daily functioning.

CAUSES OF DISSOCIATIVE DISORDERS

Dissociative disorders often emerge as adaptive responses to overwhelming events or prolonged stress, including instances of abuse, trauma, or severe stressors. These disorders serve as coping mechanisms for individuals dealing with catastrophic events, aiming to create a psychological distance from the distressing experiences.

These coping strategies can manifest in different forms, such as amnesia, where memories are blocked, out-of-body experiences, emotional numbness, and dissociative fugue, involving memory loss for specific times, people, and events. These conditions frequently co-occur with other mental health issues linked to trauma, such as depression, anxiety, PTSD, sleep disorders, eating disorders, and personality disorders.

Traumatic situations encompass a range of experiences, including:

- repeated physical, mental or sexual abuse
- an accident
- a natural disaster
- military combat
- being a victim of a crime

More examples of traumatic situations included in Chapter 2.

WHAT HAPPENS IN THE BRAIN DURING DISSOCIATION

Even though the specific neurobiological causes of dissociation are still unclear, continued research in this area could help to clarify the complexities of this psychological phenomenon and possibly pave the way for the creation of more focused therapeutic interventions as well as a more thorough understanding of the condition.

Dissociation involves a disturbance in how the brain normally integrates various cognitive functions. Recent studies using neuroimaging techniques have shown that altered brain structure and function, particularly in areas like the posteromedial cortex, may be linked to dissociative symptoms. The posteromedial cortex is important for self-awareness and integrating different cognitive processes, and disruptions in this region could contribute to the fragmentation of consciousness and identity in dissociation.

Trauma-related dissociation is a specific type characterized by profound disruptions in one's sense of self, perception, and emotions. Traumatic events can lead to a disconnection between different aspects of consciousness, resulting in a fragmented experience of reality.

Dissociative phenomena involve changes in consciousness that affect the normal integration of memory, emotions, self-awareness, body awareness, and perception of the external environment. In individuals experiencing dissociation, these elements no longer work together seamlessly, leading to a disconnection from their usual cohesive sense of self.

The process of dissociation seems to involve synchronized firing of nerve cells in the posteromedial cortex at a specific rate. This synchronized activity may trigger a series of events that disrupt the usual coordination between different brain regions, ultimately causing the characteristic symptoms of dissociation.

LONG-TERM EFFECTS OF DISSOCIATION ON THE BRAIN

When dissociation is chronic and severe, especially in the context of conditions like post-traumatic stress disorder (PTSD) and other neuropsychiatric disorders, it can have profound and lasting effects on the brain.

One significant aspect of trauma-related dissociation is the disruption of one's sense of self, perceptual experiences, and emotional responses. This can lead to a feeling of detachment from one's own emotions, thoughts, or even a sense of disconnection from the external world. Studies indicate that these dissociative symptoms are linked to changes in brain structure, although the specific neurobiological mechanisms are complicated and not fully understood.

The altered state of consciousness during dissociation can impact the normal integration of cognitive functions, affecting memory, emotions, sense of self, body awareness, and perception of the external environment. Individuals experiencing dissociation may struggle with remembering things, have difficulty recognizing their own emotions, or feel detached from their physical sensations. This fragmentation of experiences contributes to a sense of unreality and disrupts the smooth flow of information processing in the brain.

Furthermore, prolonged and intense dissociative experiences, as seen in conditions like PTSD, may lead to persistent changes in neural circuits. Research suggests that chronic dissociation could contribute to alterations in crucial brain areas, such as the hippocampus, amygdala, and prefrontal cortex, which play roles in memory, emotion regulation, and self-awareness. These changes might impact an individual's ability to cope with stress, regulate emotions, and create coherent narratives of their life experiences.

The specific mechanisms and long-term ramifications of these changes are still being researched, and more research is required to completely comprehend the impact of dissociation on the brain.

IMPACT ON DAILY LIFE

One of the primary challenges is the potential for isolation. The nature of DID often involves a sense of fragmentation within yourself, making it difficult to fully connect with others. You might feel as though certain parts of your identity are hidden or inaccessible, leading to a sense of loneliness and detachment from those around you. This can result in social withdrawal as you struggle to integrate your various identity states into a cohesive and shared experience.

For someone with DID, maintaining relationships can be especially difficult. People close to you could find it confusing and unpredictable because of your changing identities, which makes it harder for them to comprehend and relate to your experiences. Relationship problems can also result from amnesia or frequent memory loss, since friends and family may find it difficult to understand the discrepancies between your conduct and memories. This may lead to a vicious cycle of annoyance and miscommunication, which heightens the feeling of loneliness.

In the workplace, DID can pose significant hurdles. One of the disorder's main features, amnesia, can make it difficult to remember crucial details, deadlines, or discussions. This may make it difficult to execute your work and may make you feel inadequate. It can be psychologically taxing to constantly coordinate and manage various identity states, which may affect your focus and general productivity at work.

Moreover, individuals with DID often contend with co-occurring conditions such as depression and anxiety. The burden of managing multiple identities and the challenges in maintaining relationships and work commitments can exacerbate these mental health issues. Depression may stem from the isolation and frustration of living with a condition that is not well understood by society, while anxiety may arise from the constant need to navigate a world that feels unpredictable and unfamiliar.

Long-Term Effects of Dissociation

Experiencing dissociation over the long term can have profound effects on your overall well-being. As you navigate through the complexities of dissociation, various challenges may arise, impacting different aspects of your life.

One significant long-term effect is emotional dysregulation, where you may find it increasingly difficult to manage and control your emotions. You might experience intense mood swings, heightened anxiety, or persistent feelings of emptiness. This emotional turbulence can make it challenging to maintain stability in your daily life, affecting your relationships, work, and overall sense of fulfillment.

Long-term dissociation frequently comes with interpersonal issues, making it difficult to build and sustain healthy relationships. You may struggle to connect emotionally with people, making it difficult to trust and be vulnerable. These difficulties might lead to feelings of isolation and loneliness, increasing the effects on your mental health.

Low self-esteem and self-identity confusion are common outcomes of long-term dissociation. As you detach from your emotions and experiences, a sense of self can become fragmented and unclear. This may result in a diminished sense of self-worth and identity, making it difficult for you to establish a strong and positive self-image.

The persistence of dissociation can also manifest in the form of distressing flashbacks and nightmares. Unwanted memories may intrude upon your consciousness, causing emotional distress and disrupting your daily life. The recurrence of these intrusive memories can be emotionally draining, further contributing to the challenges you face in maintaining a sense of normalcy.

Additionally, the physical toll of dissociation may manifest in various health problems, such as chronic pain and fatigue. The mind-body connection is complex, and the prolonged state of dissociation can contribute to physical ailments. Persistent dissociation-related stress may lead to tension, muscle pain, and persistent fatigue, further complicating your overall well-being.

MENTAL HEALTH AND SYMPTOMS CHECKLIST

Dissociative Disorder Symptom Checklist

Symptoms	Degree (1-5)
1. Depersonalization: feeling detached from oneself, as if observing from outside.	
2. Derealization: perceiving the external environment as unreal or distorted.	
3. Gaps in memory: forgetting significant events or chunks of time.	
4. Identity confusion: uncertainty about one's identity, values, or personal characteristics.	
5. Emotional numbing: limited emotional responses or feeling emotionally "flat."	
6. Amnesia for traumatic events: inability to recall specific traumatic experiences.	
7. Flashbacks: vivid, intrusive memories or re-experiencing traumatic events.	
8. Identity alterations: noticeable shifts in personality traits, behaviors, or identity.	
9. Emotional dysregulation: difficulty managing and controlling emotions.	

10. Interpersonal difficulties: trouble forming and maintaining healthy relationships.	
11. Low self-esteem: a persistent sense of low self-worth.	
12. Chronic pain: unexplained or persistent physical pain.	
13. Fatigue: persistent and unexplained fatigue.	

Instructions:

1. Rate each symptom: Use the scale of 1 to 5 to indicate the degree to which you have experienced each symptom in the last month.

- 1 = Never
- 2 = Rarely
- 3 = Occasionally
- 4 = Frequently
- 5 = Usually

2. Be honest and reflective: Consider your experiences objectively and try to recall instances of these symptoms without judgment.

3. Review your responses: After completing the checklist, review your responses to identify patterns and clusters of symptoms.

4. Seek professional help: If you notice consistently high ratings or detect worrisome trends, it's advisable to seek advice from a mental health expert for a thorough assessment and direction.

Remember, this checklist is not a diagnostic tool, but it can serve as a helpful resource for self-reflection and as a basis for discussing your experiences with a mental health professional.

In this chapter, we explored the various types of dissociative disorders, their causes, neurobiological aspects, and impact on daily life. Understanding these disorders is crucial for providing support and developing effective treatments. In the next chapter, we will discuss and understand the relationship between childhood trauma and dissociation.

CHAPTER 2

THE LINK BETWEEN DISSOCIATION AND TRAUMA

Childhood trauma plays a crucial role in the susceptibility to dissociative disorders, particularly Dissociative Identity Disorder (DID). Extensive research has revealed that the caregiver's psychological unavailability stands out as the primary predictor of dissociation by the age of 19, explaining 19% of the variation in dissociation levels. A notable study by Ross et al. in 1991 identified that 50% of 102 individuals diagnosed with DID reported experiencing physical and sexual abuse before the age of five, emphasizing its significant contribution to DID development.

Dissociative disorders, estimated to affect one percent to five percent of the global population, with DID being a rare condition diagnosed in around one point five percent, can result in profound consequences. The manifestation of trauma-related dissociative symptoms can disrupt various aspects of life, leading to chronic diseases, suicide attempts, mental disorders, substance abuse, disability, a shortened life expectancy, and increased healthcare costs.

Recognizing the big impact of childhood trauma on mental health is crucial, urging individuals to seek appropriate treatment for addressing dissociation symptoms and other mental health issues stemming from traumatic experiences.

CHILDHOOD TRAUMA AND DISSOCIATION

Childhood trauma and dissociation are tightly intertwined, with tough experiences during early life significantly shaping the way we perceive and respond to the world around us. These traumatic incidents may have a lasting impact on our mental health. These experiences can occur in various forms, such as:

- **Physical, sexual, or emotional abuse**: This involves any form of deliberate harm inflicted upon a child, including physical violence, sexual exploitation, or psychological manipulation. For instance, physical abuse might involve hitting, kicking, or burning a child, while sexual abuse may involve molestation or rape. Emotional abuse encompasses behaviors like verbal insults, threats, or constant criticism, which undermine a child's self-esteem and emotional well-being.
- **Neglect**: Neglect occurs when a caregiver fails to provide the necessary care and support for a child's physical, emotional, or psychological needs. Examples include inadequate supervision, lack of food, shelter, or clothing, and failure to address medical or emotional needs. For instance, a child might experience neglect if they are consistently left alone for extended periods without proper care or if their basic needs are consistently unmet.
- **Witnessing violence**: Children who witness violence, whether it's between caregivers, among family members, or in their communities, can experience trauma. This

includes witnessing domestic violence, community violence, or even violence in media that's inappropriate for their age. For example, a child who regularly witnesses their parents engaging in physical altercations or who lives in a neighborhood plagued by gang violence may suffer from the effects of witnessing such events.

- **Medical trauma**: Medical trauma refers to distressing experiences related to medical procedures, treatments, or hospitalization. This can include painful medical procedures, invasive surgeries, or prolonged hospital stays. For instance, a child undergoing repeated surgeries due to a chronic illness or facing a life-threatening illness may experience significant medical trauma.

- **Loss of a loved one**: For a child, experiencing the death of a loved one can be extremely distressing, especially if it happens suddenly or unexpectedly. This loss might be due to the death of a parent, sibling, grandparent, or close friend. For example, a child who loses a parent to illness, accident, or violence may struggle to cope with feelings of grief and abandonment.

- **Natural disasters**: Natural calamities like earthquakes, hurricanes, floods, or wildfires have the potential to create extensive damage and disruption, resulting in distressing situations for children impacted by them. This includes experiencing the loss of homes, possessions, or even family members, as well as enduring the chaos and uncertainty that follow such events. For instance, a child who survives a tornado that destroys their home and community may suffer from trauma-related symptoms such as anxiety, fear, or post-traumatic stress disorder (PTSD).

Dissociation can often be a natural response to the overwhelming stress of childhood trauma. It serves as a coping mechanism, which allows us to mentally distance ourselves from the painful and distressing experiences that we endured. This protective mechanism can range from fleeting moments of detachment to more severe conditions like Dissociative Identity Disorder (DID).

The link between child abuse and dissociation lies in the adaptive nature of dissociation as a defense mechanism. Children subjected to abuse may develop dissociative tendencies as a means of shielding themselves from the intensity of their emotions and the trauma they face. By dissociating, they can create a psychological barrier that helps them endure the abuse without being completely overwhelmed by its effects.

Dissociation may manifest in a variety of ways, including brief periods of feeling disconnected from one's thoughts, feelings, or environment. At its most severe, dissociation may manifest as Dissociative Identity Disorder (DID), a disease in which people have distinct, different identities or personality states.

DID is connected with Post-Traumatic Stress Disorder (PTSD), particularly arising from prolonged and repetitive traumatic experiences, especially during childhood. The development of DID is rooted in chronic trauma, underscoring the lasting impact of adverse events on an individual's psychological well-being.

The consequences of developing dissociative disorders extend beyond personal struggles, significantly affecting various aspects of daily functioning. This interference can lead to significant public health implications, with potential outcomes including severe disruptions in mental health, social relationships, and overall well-being. Recognizing the potential severity of these consequences emphasizes the importance of addressing dissociative disorders and their underlying traumatic roots.

DEVELOPMENT ISSUES AND DISSOCIATION

High levels of dissociation have a strong impact on both behavioral problems and psychopathology, particularly in individuals who have experienced maltreatment during childhood. Dissociation, which can begin to develop from infancy, often arises within the context of stressors in the caregiver-child relationship. These stressors may manifest irrespective of direct maltreatment but are heightened in cases involving abuse or neglect. The changes observed in limbic brain regions offer insight into why early stressors, including maltreatment, elevate the risk of developing dissociation.

Childhood trauma can result in severe consequences for our mental well-being. One notable effect is the impairment of our capacity to connect with our genuine feelings, needs, and thoughts, which leads to a notable lack of self-connection. This detachment from your true self can contribute to difficulties in emotional regulation, interpersonal relationships, and overall mental health.

Maltreated children and adults experiencing dissociation may exhibit a range of behavioral problems and psychopathological symptoms. The disconnection from your true emotions and experiences, which stem from childhood trauma, can manifest in problematic behaviors and contribute to the development of psychopathological conditions. Mental health professionals working with traumatized children are increasingly diagnosing childhood and adolescent dissociative disorders. This recognition underscores the importance of addressing dissociation in the aftermath of childhood trauma to mitigate its adverse effects on mental health and overall well-being.

SYMPTOMS OF DISSOCIATION IN CHILDREN

Children experiencing dissociation may display various symptoms, and these include:

- **Crying and screaming:**

Intense crying or screaming episodes in children may signal a profound struggle in handling overwhelming emotions linked to stress or trauma. These emotional outbursts serve as visible indicators of their internal turmoil, representing a plea for help in understanding and managing their feelings effectively.

For instance, a six-year-old child, Emma, witnessed a car accident and, since then, has frequent episodes of intense crying and screaming whenever she hears loud noises or sees cars approaching. These emotional outbursts are a visible expression of her struggle to process the traumatic event she witnessed.

- **Getting scared:**

Excessive fear in certain situations can act as a sign of dissociative reactions in children. This heightened fear response may function as a self-protective mechanism, enabling them to mentally distance themselves from perceived threats. The fear may be deeply rooted in past traumatic experiences, influencing their current reactions to similar stimuli.

For instance, whenever eight-year-old Alex is near water, he becomes excessively fearful and refuses to go swimming. This heightened fear response is rooted in a past near-drowning experience, and it acts as a dissociative reaction, allowing him to mentally distance himself from perceived threats associated with water.

- **Awkward moments:**

Observing children experiencing awkward or clumsy moments provides insights into potential dissociation. These instances may manifest as a lack of coordination or absent-mindedness, reflecting a disconnect between their mental and physical states. It suggests that their focus is diverted, possibly due to underlying stressors or emotional challenges.

For instance, during a school presentation, 10-year-old Liam experiences moments of awkwardness, stumbling over his words and losing track of his thoughts. These instances of clumsiness reflect a potential dissociation, as his mental focus is diverted, possibly due to unresolved stressors or emotional challenges related to school performance.

- **Amnesia for important or traumatic events:**

The forgetting of crucial events or details known to have occurred hints at a form of memory loss associated with dissociation. This selective amnesia can be seen as a protective mechanism, shielding the child from the overwhelming emotional impact of traumatic experiences. It underscores the need to address the underlying causes for a comprehensive understanding.

For example, after witnessing a violent altercation in their neighborhood, 12-year-old Sarah seems unable to recall specific details of the incident, even though she was present. This selective amnesia serves as a protective mechanism, allowing her to shield herself from the emotional distress associated with the traumatic event.

- **Frequent dazed or trance-like states:**

Children appearing to be daydreaming or in a trance-like state may be engaging in dissociation as a coping strategy. These episodes of detachment can be seen as a conscious or subconscious effort to distance themselves from distressing thoughts or emotions. It highlights the importance of recognizing these states as potential signals of deeper emotional struggles.

For example, Timmy, a nine-year-old, often appears to be daydreaming during class, particularly when discussions turn emotional or intense. These trance-like states are a form of dissociation, enabling him to mentally distance himself from distressing thoughts or emotions that may be triggered by the classroom environment.

- **Perplexing forgetfulness:**

Forgetfulness in children, extending beyond traumatic events to various aspects of daily life, may serve as a clear sign of dissociation. This perplexing forgetfulness suggests a disruption in their cognitive processes, possibly influenced by unresolved emotional issues. Addressing this forgetfulness involves exploring the emotional landscape to identify and address the root causes.

For instance, Maya, a seven-year-old, frequently forgets simple tasks and instructions both at home and school, such as forgetting how to tie her shoes or complete basic math problems. This perplexing forgetfulness goes beyond typical absent-mindedness, suggesting a disruption in her cognitive processes likely influenced by underlying emotional issues.

- **Rapid shifts in mood or behavior:**

Sudden and significant changes in a child's mood or behavior can be indicative of dissociation. These rapid shifts may represent adaptive responses to challenging situations, showcasing the child's attempt to navigate and cope with their emotions. Understanding these fluctuations is crucial for providing targeted support to help them develop healthier coping mechanisms.

For example, James, an 11-year-old, experiences sudden and extreme mood swings, alternating between periods of excessive energy and moments of withdrawal. These rapid shifts in mood are indicative of dissociation, as he adapts to challenging situations by altering his emotional and behavioral responses as a way of coping. Understanding and addressing these fluctuations is crucial for providing appropriate support.

ADULT TRAUMA AND DISSOCIATIVE RESPONSES

Adult trauma refers to any significant and distressing experiences that occur during adulthood. Usually damaging and overpowering, these occurrences cause emotional or psychological anguish. A few instances are traumatic experiences that can take many different forms; however, the following are a few examples:

- terrorism or mass violence
- sexual or physical abuse and assault
- natural disasters
- serious car accidents
- arson or house fires
- combat or war zone exposure
- torture
- serious medical events

- domestic violence
- seeing death or dead bodies, including while at work
- experiencing or witnessing violence, such as a homicide or suicide
- unexpected death of a loved one.

In essence, adult trauma is any incident that happens after a person reaches adulthood and has a long-lasting detrimental effect on their mental and emotional health.

You may wonder: How are adult trauma and dissociative responses connected?

When you go through adult trauma, your nervous system kicks into high gear as a survival response to manage the intense distress. Dissociation comes into play as a protective mechanism, allowing you to distance yourself from the pain and fear associated with the traumatic experience. Initially, this detachment can be somewhat helpful in dealing with the immediate aftermath of trauma. However, if dissociation becomes a recurring pattern, it can impede your overall recovery and create challenges in various aspects of your life.

The connection between adult trauma and dissociative responses involves several factors:

- **Vulnerability to hyperarousal**

When you undergo a traumatic experience, your nervous system becomes more susceptible to hyperarousal, meaning it remains on high alert. This heightened state of sensitivity makes you more vulnerable to dissociative episodes. Triggers related to the traumatic event can easily activate this intensified state of arousal, causing moments of detachment and dissociation.

For instance, if you survived a car accident, your heightened sensitivity may lead to dissociation when you encounter triggers like screeching tires or witness a near-miss on the road. In these situations, your nervous system reacts strongly to reminders of the trauma, resulting in a temporary disconnection from the present moment as a coping mechanism.

- **Emotional overwhelm**

When you go through traumatic experiences as an individual, the emotions that come with it can be incredibly intense, to the point of feeling overwhelming and even unbearable. In order to deal with these overwhelming feelings, your mind might adopt a coping mechanism known as dissociation. This essentially means creating a temporary escape from the intense emotions associated with the trauma.

Dissociation works by providing a sense of detachment and numbness. It's as if you create a psychological distance from the emotions, allowing you to navigate through the emotional turmoil without being completely consumed by it. In practical terms, this might manifest as feeling emotionally disconnected or mentally distant from the events or emotions tied to the trauma.

For instance, consider someone who has been a victim of domestic violence. When faced with feelings of fear or anger triggered by the memories of that traumatic experience, they might enter a dissociative state. This could involve mentally distancing themselves from the emotions associated with the domestic violence, almost as if they are watching the events from a detached perspective. Dissociation, in this context, serves as a way for the individual to cope with the overwhelming emotional impact of the trauma they've experienced.

- **Difficulties processing memories**

When you experience traumatic events, the memories associated with them can become fragmented and difficult to process. Your mind might struggle to integrate these overwhelming experiences, and as a defense mechanism, it may resort to dissociation. This means that your mind creates a separation, preventing you from fully confronting the intense emotions linked to the traumatic events. Essentially, it's a way for your mind to shield itself from the overpowering feelings tied to those distressing memories.

For example, if you're a combat veteran, you might find yourself dissociating when faced with reminders of the battlefield. In this case, it serves as a protective measure, helping you avoid reliving the intense and distressing memories associated with your wartime experiences. The dissociation acts as a sort of mental shield, allowing you to distance yourself from the emotional impact of those traumatic events.

In general, the connection between adult trauma and dissociative responses is rooted in the nervous system's heightened state, the need to escape overwhelming emotions, and the challenge of processing traumatic memories. While dissociation may offer short-term relief, it can pose obstacles to long-term healing and functioning in daily life.

THE ROLE OF MEMORY IN DISSOCIATION

When you experience dissociation, it can significantly impact how you retrieve memories. This is because dissociation interferes with the neural mechanisms responsible for encoding memories, leading to potential dysfunction in the memory recall process. Essentially, dissociation creates a disconnect that hinders the normal functioning of memory. Imagine a person who survived a serious car accident. In the aftermath, they may experience dissociation as a way to cope with the overwhelming emotions and stress associated with the event. As a result, when they try to recall the details of the accident later on, they may struggle to piece together a coherent narrative. This difficulty in retrieving memories is a direct consequence of the dissociative response triggered by the traumatic experience.

Moreover, when dissociative symptoms take hold, you may feel a loss of control over your mental processes, including memory and attention. This lack of control can contribute to difficulties in recalling and organizing memories effectively. For instance, you might find it challenging to remember specific details or events from your past. Now consider Sam, who has endured a history of domestic abuse. The ongoing stress and fear may lead to dissociative symptoms, making him feel detached from his own thoughts and memories.

The severity of dissociative amnesia, a condition often associated with trauma, tends to align with the seriousness of the underlying causes or traumatic experiences. Those with severe dissociative amnesia may struggle to recover memories, which can have significant effects on their ability to build and maintain relationships. The impact of memory loss can extend to various aspects of life, hindering social connections and emotional well-being. Imagine a war veteran who has difficulty remembering significant portions of their military service. This memory loss can have profound implications for their relationships, as they may find it hard to connect with others who were part of their shared history.

Chronic dissociation and state dissociation, which involve ongoing and temporary disruptions in awareness, respectively, have been linked to diminished performance on cognitive measures. This includes difficulties in attention, executive functioning, and memory. Now, think about a person dealing with chronic dissociation. In their daily life, they might experience moments of spacing out or feeling disconnected from reality. During these episodes, they may struggle to concentrate, make decisions, or remember important details. This can impact their work performance, relationships, and overall cognitive functioning.

Additionally, there is a noteworthy connection between trauma, dissociation, lower cognitive abilities, and an increased likelihood of developing false memories. This means that, under the influence of trauma and dissociation, you may be more susceptible to forming memories that did not actually occur. This further complicates the already intricate relationship between dissociation and memory, highlighting the complex ways in which these factors can intertwine and influence one another. A person who has undergone a traumatic event and subsequently experienced dissociation may be more susceptible to developing false memories. For instance, they might recall events differently or even remember things that never happened.

PERSONAL EXPERIENCE

Since I was a very young child, as far back as I can remember, severe dissociation has been a constant presence in my life. Day after day, I find myself lost in a surreal world, unsure if I'm dreaming or awake, feeling detached from my own body as if I'm watching my life unfold on a distant screen like a movie. This perplexing experience would consume at least an hour every day, and often much more, to the point where I questioned the reality of my own existence.

Growing up, I thought this was a normal part of everyone's life until one day, around the age of 10 or 11, I had a particularly intense dissociation episode in the presence of friends. When they questioned what was happening, I casually explained, "You know that feeling when you think you're dreaming, and you can't tell if you're awake or not? That's just what's happening now." Their puzzled expressions made me realize that not everyone shared this bewildering aspect of their reality.

As the years went by, my dissociation persisted, weaving its way into the fabric of my everyday life. The challenges it presented made it difficult for me to hold down a job or maintain stable relationships. The impact of this dissociative experience was tangible and, at times, overwhelming.

The perplexity of my condition led me to question its origins. Why am I this way? Online searches often pointed to early childhood trauma as the root cause, but my memories of those early years held no traumatic events. My adolescence was undoubtedly tumultuous, marked by trauma, but my dissociation predated those turbulent years.

This realization sparked a fear within me—a fear that I might be carrying repressed memories from my childhood, that I might have endured abuse without conscious recollection. Nightmares haunted my sleep, leaving me disturbed and uncertain about the authenticity of these troubling memories. The line between reality and the tricks of my own mind blurred, leaving me in a state of perpetual unease.

I find myself grappling with the questions that linger in the shadows of my consciousness. Has my consistent and severe dissociation since childhood truly escaped the shadow of trauma, or is there a hidden past that my mind is protecting me from? The uncertainty looms large, and the search for answers continues, marking a journey through the complexities of my own mind.

In this chapter, we explored the intricate link between childhood trauma and dissociation, revealing the profound impact of distressing events on the developing brain. Emphasizing dissociation's protective role, we discussed its manifestations in both childhood and adulthood, highlighting symptoms and long-term consequences. Personal stories illuminated diverse forms of abuse and unstable environments as triggers for dissociation. The chapter underscores the significance of early intervention in recognizing and addressing dissociation. In the next chapter, we will gain a comprehensive understanding of Dissociative Identity Disorder (DID) versus schizophrenia and Borderline Personality Disorder (BPD).

CHAPTER 3

DIAGNOSING THE DISORDER

In addition to DID and dissociative amnesia, another significant condition within the spectrum of dissociative disorders is depersonalization-derealization disorder. While DID involves the presence of multiple distinct identities or personality states, and dissociative amnesia revolves around memory gaps, depersonalization-derealization disorder is characterized by a persistent sense of detachment from oneself (depersonalization) and the external world (derealization). In most cases, DID is mistaken for these other mental disorders due to the overlapping symptoms it shares with conditions like depression, anxiety, and Post-Traumatic stress Disorder (PTSD). These shared symptoms make it challenging to distinguish DID from other mental health issues. Some of the common symptoms that may overlap include changes in sleep patterns and appetite, mood swings, withdrawal from social activities, a decline in functioning at work or school, problems with concentration and memory, increased sensitivity to stimuli, a sense of disconnection from oneself or surroundings, illogical thinking, nervousness, and unusual behavior.

One significant factor contributing to the misdiagnosis is the protective mechanism of dissociation. Dissociation can act as a defense mechanism for individuals who have experienced childhood trauma. It allows them to detach from the intense emotions, pain, and fear associated with traumatic experiences. However, this protective mechanism can make it challenging to identify the underlying trauma, leading to the misdiagnosis of the condition. Clinicians may focus on treating the presenting symptoms without recognizing the dissociative aspect of the disorder.

In essence, the shared symptoms with other mental health disorders and the role of dissociation as a protective mechanism make it difficult to accurately diagnose DID. It requires a thorough understanding of the individual's history, experiences, and a careful examination of their symptoms to differentiate DID from other mental health conditions and to identify the potential underlying trauma that may be driving the dissociative responses.

DID VERSUS SCHIZOPHRENIA

DID and schizophrenia are distinct mental health disorders that might be mistakenly linked because they share certain overlapping symptoms. It is crucial to recognize and understand the differences between them to provide appropriate and effective treatment. Here are some key differences:

Multiple Identities

Individuals diagnosed with DID demonstrate the existence of several distinct identity states, commonly referred to as alternate identities or alters. These alters can differ significantly from one another, possessing distinct characteristics, memories, and ways of engaging with the surroundings. The shifts between these identities are frequently associated with memory lapses, and each identity may lack awareness of the others.

In contrast, individuals with schizophrenia do not have multiple distinct identities. Instead, they experience disruptions in thought processes, emotions, and perceptions. Symptoms of schizophrenia may include hallucinations (perceiving things that are not present) and delusions (strongly held false beliefs), but these do not involve the presence of separate identities.

Causes

DID often emerges as a consequence of severe and prolonged trauma, particularly during childhood. Traumatic experiences prompt the development of DID as a coping mechanism, enabling individuals to compartmentalize their overwhelming emotions and memories. In response to trauma, individuals with DID create distinct identity states, commonly known as alters, each possessing unique characteristics and memories. This compartmentalization serves as a means to manage the emotional distress associated with traumatic events, resulting in the manifestation of multiple identities within the individual.

On the other hand, schizophrenia is influenced by a different set of factors. Genetic and neurodevelopmental elements are deemed more significant contributors to the onset of schizophrenia. While environmental stressors may play a role, the primary influence is believed to be biological in nature, involving abnormalities in brain structure and neurotransmitter function. Unlike DID, where the development is closely linked to coping with trauma, schizophrenia's origins are deeply rooted in the complex interplay of genetic predispositions and neurobiological factors, leading to disturbances in thought processes, emotions, and perceptions. Understanding these distinct causal pathways is essential for developing targeted and effective treatment strategies for each mental health condition.

Treatment

DID is generally considered a developmental disorder and is more responsive to psychotherapy. Treatment aims to integrate the different identity states, fostering communication and cooperation among them. Psychotherapy also addresses the underlying trauma that led to the development of DID, helping individuals achieve a more cohesive sense of self.

Schizophrenia treatment typically combines antipsychotic medication with psychosocial interventions.Medications help manage symptoms like hallucinations and delusions by regulating neurotransmitter imbalances. Psychosocial treatments may include various forms of therapy, support groups, and vocational rehabilitation to enhance overall functioning and quality of life.

It is important to note that distinguishing between DID and schizophrenia can be challenging because both conditions may present with symptoms of psychosis, such as distorted thinking and altered perceptions of reality.

BORDERLINE PERSONALITY DISORDER (BPD) VERSUS DID

Borderline Personality Disorder (BPD) is a mental health condition characterized by various symptoms that collectively affect a person's emotional well-being, self-perception, and interpersonal relationships. Here's an elaboration on the specified aspects of BPD:

- **Emotional dysregulation and impulsivity:**

Individuals with BPD often find it difficult to control their emotions. This difficulty can result in experiencing strong and quickly shifting emotional states, making it hard for them to maintain a stable emotional balance. Impulsivity is another common trait, where they act on their urges or impulses without carefully thinking about the possible outcomes. People with BPD may engage in impulsive actions like reckless driving, substance abuse, or self-harm, reflecting the challenges they face in managing their emotions and behaviors.

- **Unstable self-image and relationships:**

BPD is associated with a pervasive and unstable sense of self. Individuals may experience frequent shifts in self-identity, values, and goals. Their relationships with others are also marked by instability. Intense and tumultuous relationships can occur, where individuals may idealize someone one moment and then devalue them the next. Fear of abandonment might drive desperate actions to prevent actual or perceived rejection.

- **Rapid mood swings and fluctuating sense of self:**

Rapid and unpredictable mood swings are a hallmark of BPD. Individuals may experience intense happiness, anger, or sadness in short periods, often without an apparent trigger. The sense of self can fluctuate, contributing to an overall feeling of emptiness and confusion about one's identity.

- **Self-destructive behaviors and suicidal ideation:**

Individuals with BPD commonly show self-destructive behaviors like physical self-harm, substance abuse, or risky actions, often stemming from intense emotional turmoil and hopelessness. In severe cases, this may lead to contemplation or planning of self-harm or suicide due to emotional instability. Offering timely support and intervention is crucial for addressing their mental health challenges.

- **Difficulty managing stress and maintaining relationships:**

Individuals with BPD often find it challenging to cope with stress in a healthy manner. Everyday stressors may trigger intense emotional reactions and contribute to a sense of overwhelm. Maintaining stable and fulfilling relationships can be difficult due to the interpersonal challenges associated with BPD. Fear of abandonment, coupled with emotional volatility, can strain connections with others.

So, what is the difference between the two?

- **Identity issues:**

In DID, individuals experience the coexistence of two or more distinct identities or personality states, each with its own way of interacting with the world, consciousness, and memories. These identities often take control of the person's behavior at different times.

BPD, on the other hand, involves a more generalized instability in self-image and identity. Individuals with BPD may struggle with a sense of self, experience rapid shifts in self-identity, and have a chronic fear of abandonment. However, these identity issues are not characterized by distinct and separate personalities as in DID.

- **Causes:**

DID is frequently associated with a background of significant trauma, usually experienced during childhood. The formation of separate identities is considered a coping strategy to manage intense and distressing situations, such as instances of abuse or neglect.

BPD is influenced by a combination of factors, including genetic predisposition, neurochemical imbalances, and environmental factors such as early-life adversity or trauma. While trauma can be a contributing factor, it is not as directly associated with the development of separate identities as it is in DID.

- **Treatment:**

Treatment for Borderline Personality Disorder often involves psychotherapy, with Dialectical Behavior Therapy (DBT) being a common and effective approach. DBT helps individuals regulate their emotions, improve interpersonal relationships, and develop coping mechanisms.

Effectively addressing DID usually involves a blend of medications and psychosocial therapies. The therapeutic approach centers on achieving integration, aiming to consolidate distinct identities into a more unified sense of self. While medications may be prescribed to alleviate specific symptoms like mood swings or anxiety, they are not the primary means of treating the fundamental identity-related challenges.

EARLY DIAGNOSTIC BENCHMARKS

Diagnosing dissociative disorders involves a comprehensive approach that encompasses both physical and mental health examinations. The physical exam is crucial in diagnosing dissociative disorders, primarily to rule out physical conditions that may be causing the symptoms. During this examination, a healthcare professional, typically a doctor, carefully assesses your physical health by conducting a thorough examination, discussing your symptoms, and reviewing your medical history. Specific tests may be administered to exclude physical factors that might manifest as dissociative symptoms, such as memory loss or a feeling of detachment from reality.

Blood tests are one specific test that may be performed in order to rule out the chance that the dissociative symptoms are caused by any physical reasons. For example, a blood test could be used to identify deficiencies in essential vitamins or minerals. If someone lacks certain nutrients crucial for overall health, it may lead to symptoms that resemble those associated with dissociative disorders. One specific example is a deficiency in vitamin B12, which is essential for neurological function. A person with low levels of vitamin B12 might experience fatigue, confusion, and memory problems, which could be mistaken for dissociative symptoms. Another example could be testing for thyroid function. Hypothyroidism, a state characterized by insufficient production of thyroid hormones by the thyroid gland, can display symptoms like fatigue, concentration difficulties, and mood changes. These symptoms might be mistakenly attributed to dissociative disorders without considering the potential underlying thyroid issues. Conditions ruled out through this process may include head injuries, certain brain diseases, severe sleep deprivation, and substance abuse like drug or alcohol use.

In addition to the physical exam, a mental health exam is crucial for diagnosing dissociative disorders. This examination focuses on evaluating your mental and emotional well-being. A mental health professional engages in conversations with you to explore thoughts, feelings, behaviors, and specific symptoms related to dissociation. Permission may be sought to gather information from family members or other relevant sources for a more comprehensive understanding. Acknowledging the speaker's emotions, paying attention to body language, and allowing the individual to guide the conversation are integral aspects of the mental health exam. This comprehensive assessment ensures a nuanced understanding of dissociative symptoms and aids in formulating an accurate diagnosis. Combining both physical and mental health examinations is key to a thorough diagnostic process for dissociative disorders, allowing for a holistic approach to the individual's well-being.

BASK MODEL

The BASK model provides a framework for understanding various aspects of dissociative disorders, particularly DID. When a traumatic incident occurs, many people experience significant dissociation as a form of self-protection. It helps to compartmentalize the experience, or to place portions of it far outside of conscious awareness, where they cannot be reached. It would be too upsetting to keep fresh in your memory, or even easily available, when you're trying to get to work or simply make supper. However, memories are composed of a diverse range of mental, physical, emotional, and sensory experiences! Simply said, we classify them into four categories: behavior, affect, sensory, and knowledge. We break down each of these further in the graphics below.

- **Behavior:**

This involves observing and recognizing the actions or behaviors of a person with dissociative disorders. In DID, it may include the emergence of different personalities, each with its own distinct behaviors. The focus is on what the person physically did or felt compelled to do in response to a particular situation. For instance, did they hide, run away, attack, or exhibit any other specific behavior?

- **Affect:**

Affect pertains to the emotional experiences of individuals with dissociative disorders. In DID, different alters may have unique emotional states. This aspect explores the emotions felt during a specific moment, even those that might have been suppressed or turned off. Questions revolve around whether the person felt sad, afraid, angry, calm, or any other emotion during that particular experience.

- **Sensory:**

Sensory experiences refer to the sensations felt by individuals with dissociative disorders. In DID, different alters may have distinct sensory preferences or experiences, including sounds, textures, tastes, or physical sensations. This aspect looks into what the person felt in their body, such as a racing heart, physical pain, numbness, or specific sensory details like smells, sounds, tastes, and external feelings against the skin.

- **Knowledge:**

Knowledge involves the cognitive aspects of dissociative disorders, encompassing the individual's awareness of their alters and their understanding of the dissociative process. Here, the focus is on what the person was intellectually aware of at the time, including the who, what, when, where, and how of the situation. It also explores their thoughts and beliefs during that moment, even if those thoughts were later found to be incorrect.

DISSOCIATIVE EXPERIENCE SCALE (DES)

DES is a tool that you can use to assess how often you experience dissociative episodes. Developed by Eve Bernstein Carlson and Frank W. Putnam in 1993, this questionnaire comprises 28 questions. These questions cover various dissociative experiences like amnesia, depersonalization, and derealization.

When you fill out the DES, you're asked to rate how frequently you encounter these dissociative episodes on a scale from 0 to 100. This scale helps capture the severity and prevalence of your dissociative symptoms. It's a valuable instrument used not only in clinical settings, but also in research contexts to understand the presence and intensity of dissociative experiences.

Dissociative Experiences Assessment

Instructions: There are 28 questions on experiences related to your daily life in this questionnaire. We would want to know how frequently you encounter these situations. Please indicate the frequency with which these incidents occur in your life when you are not under the influence of drugs or alcohol. In order to reply, write the corresponding number on the scale from 0% to 100% to represent the proportion of time you have the experience.

1. Some people experience not remembering what happened during all or part of a trip. How often does this happen to you?

   ____

2. Some people realize they did not hear part or all of what was said while listening to someone. How often does this happen to you?

   ____

3. Some people find themselves in a place without any idea of how they got there. How often does this happen to you?

   ____

4. Some people find themselves dressed in clothes they don't remember putting on. How often does this happen to you?

   ____

5. Some people find new things among their belongings that they don't remember buying. How often does this happen to you?

   ____

6. Some people are approached by strangers calling them by another name or insisting they have met before. How often does this happen to you?

   ____

7. Some people feel as though they are standing next to themselves, watching themselves do something. How often does this happen to you?

   ____

8. Some people do not recognize friends or family members. How often does this happen to you?

   ____

9. Some people have no memory of important events in their lives. How often does this happen to you?

____

10. Some people are accused of lying when they don't think they have lied. How often does this happen to you?

____

11. Some people look in a mirror and do not recognize themselves. How often does this happen to you?

____

12. Some people feel that people, objects, and the world around them are not real. How often does this happen to you?

____

13. Some people feel that their body does not seem to belong to them. How often does this happen to you?

____

14. Some people vividly remember a past event and feel as if they are reliving it. How often does this happen to you?

____

15. Some people are unsure whether remembered events really happened or were just dreams. How often does this happen to you?

____

16. Some people find familiar places strange and unfamiliar. How often does this happen to you?

____

17. Some people become so absorbed in a story that they are unaware of events around them. How often does this happen to you?

____

18. Some people get so involved in a fantasy or daydream that it feels real. How often does this happen to you?

____

19. Some people are able to ignore pain in certain situations. How often does this happen to you?

____

20. Some people sit staring off into space, unaware of the passage of time. How often does this happen to you?

____

21. Some people talk out loud to themselves when alone. How often does this happen to you?

____

22. Some people act so differently in different situations that they feel like two different people. How often does this happen to you?

____

23. Some people can do things with amazing ease in specific situations. How often does this happen to you?

____

24. Some people cannot remember whether they have done something or just thought about it. How often does this happen to you?

____

25. Some people find evidence of doing things they don't remember. How often does this happen to you?

____

26. Some people find writings, drawings, or notes among their belongings that they don't remember creating. How often does this happen to you?

____

27. Some people hear voices inside their head telling them to do things or commenting on their actions. How often does this happen to you?

____

28. Some people feel as if they are looking at the world through a fog, making people and objects seem unclear.

How often does this happen to you?

───────────────────────────────

Note: Please be honest in your responses, indicating the true frequency of these experiences in your daily life.

SOMATOFORM DISSOCIATION QUESTIONNAIRE

The Somatoform Dissociation Questionnaire (SDQ) is a self-report instrument designed to assess somatoform dissociation. Somatoform dissociation refers to disruptions in the normally integrated functions of consciousness, memory, identity, and perception that are related to physical symptoms. It is a concept often associated with dissociative disorders.

The SDQ was developed by Nijenhuis, Spinhoven, Van Dyck, Van der Hart, and Vanderlinden and is commonly used in the field of psychiatry and psychology. It consists of a set of questions that individuals answer to provide information about their experiences of dissociation in relation to physical symptoms. The questionnaire aims to measure various aspects of somatoform dissociation, such as derealization, depersonalization, and gaps in consciousness.

It's important to note that the SDQ is not a standalone diagnostic tool; rather, it is usually utilized in a clinical setting. It is frequently used by mental health specialists as a component of a thorough evaluation to assist determine the type and degree of dissociative symptoms in specific people. It is advised that you use or interpret the SDQ under the supervision of a licensed mental health professional if you are considering doing so. They can offer relevant context and interpretation based on the patient's overall clinical presentation.

Dissociative Symptom Assessment Questionnaire (DSAQ-20)

Please provide your name, date, age, sex, and marital status.

Name: ___________________

Date: ___________________

Age: ___________________

Sex: *female / male*

Marital status:

- □ single
- □ married
- □ living together
- □ divorced
- □ widower/widow

Education: __________ (number of years)

This questionnaire is designed to assess various dissociative symptoms or experiences you may have had in the past year. Please indicate the extent to which each statement applies to you by circling the appropriate number. Additionally, if a symptom applies to you, indicate whether a physician has connected it with a physical disease by circling YES or NO.

Example:

Sometimes my teeth chatter

- □ 1 - Not at all
- □ 2 - A little
- □ 3 - Moderately
- □ 4 - Quite a bit
- □ 5 - Extremely

Is the physical cause known?

   □ NO

   □ YES, namely ________________

Dissociative Symptom Assessment:

1. I have trouble urinating

   □ 1   □ 2   □ 3   □ 4   □ 5

Is the physical cause known?

□ NO

□ YES, namely ________________

2. I dislike tastes that I usually like (women: at times other than pregnancy or monthly periods)

   □ 1   □ 2   □ 3   □ 4   □ 5

Is the physical cause known?

□ NO

□ YES, namely ________________

3. I hear sounds from nearby as if they were coming from far away

   □ 1   □ 2   □ 3   □ 4   □ 5

Is the physical cause known?

□ NO

□ YES, namely ________________

4. I have pain while urinating

☐ 1   ☐ 2   ☐ 3   ☐ 4   ☐ 5
Is the physical cause known?
☐ NO
☐ YES, namely _______________________

5. My body, or a part of it, feels numb

☐ 1   ☐ 2   ☐ 3   ☐ 4   ☐ 5
Is the physical cause known?
☐ NO
☐ YES, namely _______________________

6. People and things look bigger than usual

☐ 1   ☐ 2   ☐ 3   ☐ 4   ☐ 5
Is the physical cause known?
☐ NO
☐ YES, namely _______________________

7. I have an attack that resembles an epileptic seizure

☐ 1   ☐ 2   ☐ 3   ☐ 4   ☐ 5
Is the physical cause known?
☐ NO
☐ YES, namely _______________________

8. My body, or a part of it, is insensitive to pain

□ 1 □ 2 □ 3 □ 4 □ 5
Is the physical cause known?
□ NO
□ YES, namely _________________

9. I dislike smells that I usually like

□ 1 □ 2 □ 3 □ 4 □ 5
Is the physical cause known?
□ NO
□ YES, namely _________________

10. I feel pain in my genitals (at times other than sexual intercourse)

□ 1 □ 2 □ 3 □ 4 □ 5
Is the physical cause known?
□ NO
□ YES, namely _________________

11. I cannot hear for a while (as if I am deaf)

□ 1 □ 2 □ 3 □ 4 □ 5
Is the physical cause known?
□ NO
□ YES, namely _________________

12. I cannot see for a while (as if I am blind)

□ 1   □ 2   □ 3   □ 4   □ 5
Is the physical cause known?
□ NO
□ YES, namely _______________________

13. I see things around me differently than usual

□ 1   □ 2   □ 3   □ 4   □ 5
Is the physical cause known?
□ NO
□ YES, namely _______________________

14. I am able to smell much BETTER or WORSE than I usually do (even though I do not have a cold)

□ 1   □ 2   □ 3   □ 4   □ 5
Is the physical cause known?
□ NO
□ YES, namely _______________________

15. It is as if my body, or a part of it, has disappeared

□ 1   □ 2   □ 3   □ 4   □ 5
Is the physical cause known?
□ NO
□ YES, namely _______________________

16. I cannot swallow, or can swallow only with great effort

☐ 1   ☐ 2   ☐ 3   ☐ 4   ☐ 5
Is the physical cause known?
☐ NO
☐ YES, namely ________________

17. I cannot sleep for nights on end, but remain very active during daytime

☐ 1   ☐ 2   ☐ 3   ☐ 4   ☐ 5
Is the physical cause known?
☐ NO
☐ YES, namely ________________

18. I cannot speak (or only with great effort) or I can only whisper

☐ 1   ☐ 2   ☐ 3   ☐ 4   ☐ 5
Is the physical cause known?
☐ NO
☐ YES, namely ________________

19. I am paralyzed for a while

☐ 1 ☐ 2 ☐ 3 ☐ 4 ☐ 5
Is the physical cause known?
☐ NO
☐ YES, namely ________________

20. I grow stiff for a while

☐ 1   ☐ 2   ☐ 3   ☐ 4   ☐ 5
Is the physical cause known?
☐ NO
☐ YES, namely _________________

Please check that you have responded to all 20 statements. Thank you for your cooperation.

Scoring and interpretation:

The individual item scores of the DSAQ-20 are added together to create the score, which runs from 20 to 100. This survey serves as a screening tool, and depending on the results, more evaluation can be recommended.

- **>50 range:** Suggestive of Dissociative Identity Disorder (DID)
- **40 - 50 range:** Indicative of Dissociative Disorder Not Otherwise Specified (DDNOS)
- **30s range:** Associated with Eating Disorders
- **<30 range:** Possibly related to Bipolar Disorder or other non-dissociative conditions (anxiety, depression, adjustment disorder)

Note: Scores are influenced by self-reported physical and sexual trauma, especially those occurring between zero and six years of age.

DAILY ENERGY VERSUS MOOD TRACKER

Instructions:

Use this tracker daily to monitor your energy levels and mood. By keeping a record of symptoms, medication, nutrition, and exercise, you can identify patterns and triggers of dissociation. Fill in the information below each day and reflect on any correlations you notice over time.

Date: ______________________

Energy Level:

(On a scale of 1-10, 1 being very low energy and 10 being high energy)

____

Mood: (Choose one: Very Sad, sad, neutral, happy, very happy)

____

Symptoms:

(List any physical or mental symptoms you experience, such as fatigue, headaches, anxiety, etc.)

____

____

____

____

____

Medication:

(List any medications you take and note if there were any changes
or missed doses)

Nutrition:

(Record what you ate and drank throughout the day, including
snacks and beverages)

Exercise:

(Detail any physical activity you engaged in, including duration and intensity)

____

____

____

____

____

Reflections:

(Take a moment to reflect on your day. Were there any notable events or stressors? How did your energy and mood fluctuate throughout the day?)

____

____

____

____

____

~

Tips for effective tracking:

1. Be consistent: Fill out the tracker at the same time each day.
2. Be honest: Record your feelings and experiences accurately.

3. Look for patterns: Pay attention to recurring themes or triggers.
4. Seek support: Share your findings with a trusted friend, therapist, or healthcare provider.
5. Adjust as needed: Use the insights gained to make changes to your routine or treatment plan.

Remember, tracking is a tool for self-awareness and empowerment. Take care of yourself and prioritize your well-being.

Please note that this tracker should not be used in place of expert medical advice; it is meant only for personal use. For individualized advice, speak with a healthcare professional.

PERSONAL STORIES: CELEBRITIES DEALING WITH DISSOCIATIVE DISORDER

Adam Duritz

He is a well-known American songwriter, musician, film producer, and record producer, famous for being the lead vocalist and frontman of the highly acclaimed alternative rock band Counting Crows. Duritz's battle with dissociative identity disorder, which affects his relationships with friends and family, is acknowledged by many of his fans. To address his condition, he chose to seek professional help and has found a medication that effectively controls his disorder, enabling him to lead a more manageable life.

Truddi Chase

Truddi Chase, a well-known author, also grapples with dissociative identity disorder. In 1987, he authored the book titled *When Rabbit Howls*. The origins of his disorder trace back to a history of violent and sexual abuse endured during childhood. Personality disorders like these frequently emerge as a result of various forms of abuse.

Marilyn Monroe

Marilyn Monroe, the iconic American model, actress, and singer, gained fame as a sex symbol early in her showbiz career. Despite her legendary status, Monroe faced challenges with dissociative identity disorder, a condition inherited from her maternal side. Raised in foster care, her upbringing had profound negative impacts. Speculation surrounds the idea that this disorder may have been a factor in her premature death due to a prescription drug overdose.

Hershel Walker

Renowned for his prowess in both mixed martial arts and football, Hershel Walker, a standout player for the Philadelphia Eagles, has left an indelible mark on the sports world. Despite his remarkable achievements, Walker faced the challenge of undiagnosed dissociative identity disorder, a condition that clouded even significant moments, such as winning the Heisman Trophy.

In an effort to shed light on his experiences with this disorder, Walker authored the book Breaking Free: My Life With *Dissociative Identity Disorder*. Through the process of sharing his journey, Walker not only raised awareness about his condition but also found a renewed sense of positivity. His book became a testament to his resilience as he actively strives to confront and overcome the challenges posed by dissociative identity disorder.

In conclusion, diagnosing dissociative disorders, such as Dissociative Identity Disorder (DID), is challenging due to symptom overlap with depression, anxiety, and PTSD. The protective mechanism of dissociation complicates accurate identification, leading to misdiagnoses. Distinguishing DID from conditions like schizophrenia and Borderline Personality Disorder (BPD) is crucial for effective intervention. The BASK model, along with tools like the Dissociative Experience Scale (DES) and Somatoform Dissociation Questionnaire, aids in understanding. Early diagnostic benchmarks, including both physical and mental health examinations, are essential for a holistic approach. In the next chapter, you will discover a comprehensive exploration of treatment options for managing dissociation.

CHAPTER 4

TREATMENT OPTIONS

Creating a secure treatment environment is essential for addressing dissociation, a defense mechanism developed to cope with overwhelming emotions, especially after traumatic experiences. While dissociation can be adaptive temporarily, frequent and intense occurrences can hinder concentration, learning, memory, and interpersonal connections. Treatment focuses on creating a safe and relaxed setting, with the primary goal of reducing dissociation and integrating mind functions. Psychotherapy, lacking robust empirical evidence across various approaches, remains pivotal. Selecting an appropriate therapist is crucial, especially in complex cases requiring a multidisciplinary treatment team.

TREATMENT OPTIONS

The primary treatment options for dissociation are psychotherapy and, in certain situations, medication. The primary treatment for dissociative disorders is talk therapy, sometimes known as psychotherapy, which is discussing the disorder and associated difficulties with a mental health expert. Some key treatment options include:

Psychotherapy

Psychotherapy is the major therapy used to treat dissociative disorders. Its importance lies in helping people understand the underlying reasons of their illness and in helping them develop new coping strategies for handling difficult and stressful circumstances. It is impossible to overestimate the significance of this therapeutic strategy, since it focuses on helping patients create healthy coping mechanisms for the obstacles in their lives, as well as identifying the underlying causes of dissociation. The goal of this treatment is to enhance people's mental health in a comprehensive and long-lasting way by addressing the underlying problems and offering coping mechanisms.

Types of Psychotherapies for Dissociation

- **Talking therapy**

Talking therapy, or psychoanalytic therapy, is a foundational aspect of psychotherapy that centers around open and supportive conversations between you and a mental health professional. In this therapeutic approach, you have the opportunity to express your thoughts and emotions in a secure and non-judgmental environment. This form of therapy proves particularly beneficial in addressing dissociative disorders, as it encourages you to look into self-reflection and explore the underlying issues contributing to your condition. By providing a safe space for open dialogue, talking therapy fosters an atmosphere where you can openly communicate your ideas and feelings, facilitating a deeper understanding of the root causes of dissociation. The emphasis on introspection and the exploration of underlying problems distinguishes talking therapy as a valuable and effective tool in the treatment of dissociative disorders.

- **Cognitive-Behavioral Therapy (CBT)**

Cognitive-Behavioral Therapy (CBT) is a widely utilized therapeutic method focused on identifying and changing negative thought patterns and behaviors. In this process, you are actively involved in the journey of self-discovery and transformation. CBT serves as a guide, helping you recognize distorted perceptions that might be influencing your outlook. By encouraging you to question dysfunctional beliefs, the therapy opens doors to a more realistic and balanced understanding of yourself and your surroundings. Moreover, CBT supports you in cultivating positive cognitive and behavioral reactions, fostering a proactive and adaptive response to various life situations. As you engage in this therapeutic process, the aim is to establish a stronger connection between your thoughts, emotions, and behaviors, ultimately granting you the tools to regain control over the narrative of your life.

- **Dialectical-Behavioral Therapy (DBT)**

Dialectical-Behavioral Therapy (DBT), originally developed to address borderline personality disorder, has proven effective in managing dissociative symptoms, offering a valuable therapeutic approach tailored to individual needs. In the realm of DBT, you, as the individual undergoing therapy, engage in a combination of cognitive-behavioral techniques and mindfulness strategies. This unique blend places a significant emphasis on fostering both acceptance and change. Throughout the therapeutic process, DBT guides you to recognize and endure distress, promoting a mindful approach to your emotions and experiences. Simultaneously, it encourages you to actively work towards positive behavioral transformations, empowering you to navigate challenges and enhance overall well-being. The dual focus on acceptance and change in DBT creates a comprehensive and adaptive framework for addressing dissociative symptoms and promoting personal growth.

- **Psychodynamic psychotherapy**

Psychodynamic psychotherapy, grounded in psychoanalytic principles, is an approach that explores unconscious processes and unresolved conflicts contributing to your dissociative symptoms. In this therapeutic method, the focus is on fostering insight into your past experiences and understanding how they influence your current functioning. By addressing unconscious factors, psychodynamic psychotherapy seeks to unveil the roots of dissociative symptoms. This process not only allows you to gain a deeper understanding of yourself, but also facilitates the connection of fragmented aspects of your identity. The goal is to promote integration, enabling you to form a more cohesive sense of self. Through this exploration, psychodynamic psychotherapy aims to empower you to navigate and understand the complexities of your internal experiences, ultimately fostering personal growth and psychological well-being.

- **Eye Movement Desensitization and Reprocessing (EMDR) therapy**

EMDR is a type of psychotherapy that aims to alleviate distress caused by traumatic memories. Individuals suffering from trauma-related dissociative disorders may benefit most from this therapy approach. During an EMDR session, you actively engage in guided eye movements while recalling distressing memories. This intentional focus, guided by the therapist, serves to facilitate the reprocessing of traumatic experiences. As you undergo this process, the emotional intensity tied to these memories is gradually reduced. The aim is to lessen the emotional charge, making it more manageable, and ultimately fostering adaptive integration. In essence, EMDR empowers you to navigate and transform the impact of traumatic memories, contributing to a more balanced and integrated emotional well-being.

- **Schema therapy**

Schema therapy is a therapeutic approach that centers on recognizing and addressing maladaptive patterns, known as schemas, that originated during your childhood and contribute to dissociative symptoms. The focus is on understanding how early experiences may have shaped your current cognitive and behavioral patterns. By combining cognitive, behavioral, and experiential techniques, this approach aims to empower you in modifying entrenched patterns. Through this process, you work towards promoting healthier ways of thinking and behaving, fostering a positive shift in your overall mental well-being. The personalized nature of schema therapy encourages you to explore and understand the origins of these patterns, empowering you to actively participate in the transformative journey towards greater emotional resilience and adaptive functioning.

Some of these will be discussed in detail throughout this chapter.

Preparing for Your Appointment

When getting ready for your psychological therapy appointment, it's essential to proactively engage in self-reflection. Take the time to consider your thoughts and emotions, and make an effort to identify specific concerns or topics that you want to discuss during the session. Jotting down these points beforehand can help ensure that you make the most of your time with the therapist. Additionally, reflect on any recurring patterns or triggers you've noticed in your experiences, as this self-awareness can provide valuable insights for both you and your therapist.

What You Can Do

Before your appointment, create a checklist that includes:

- Any symptoms you're experiencing, including recent behaviors that have caused confusion or concern for either yourself or your loved ones.
- Essential personal details, such as major stressors or recent life changes. Additionally, jot down significant events from your past, including childhood experiences that have contributed to physical or emotional issues. If there are periods of your life that you can't recall, indicate the timeframe and provide any details you can recall leading up to the memory loss.
- Your medical history, encompassing any physical or mental health conditions you've been diagnosed with. Make sure to include a list of medications, vitamins, herbs, or supplements you're currently taking, along with their respective dosages.

- Prepare a set of questions to maximize the efficiency of your appointment and ensure that all your concerns are addressed thoroughly.

Choosing a Therapist

Selecting a therapist is a key decision that has a big impact on the outcome of your therapeutic journey. It is critical to perform extensive research on potential therapists, taking into account elements such as their specialty and treatment methods. Reviewing online profiles, testimonials, and obtaining recommendations might provide useful information. When making this decision, trust your instincts, as selecting a therapist who understands your needs and preferences is critical to building a healthy therapeutic partnership.

Here are the questions you can consider asking your therapist to enhance the effectiveness of your therapy sessions:

1. What is probably triggering my symptoms or condition?
2. What alternative causes should be considered?
3. How will you arrive at a diagnosis for my condition?
4. Is my condition expected to be temporary or long-lasting?
5. What treatments do you suggest for my condition?
6. To what extent can I anticipate an improvement in my symptoms with treatment?
7. How do you plan to track my progress?
8. I have additional health conditions. How can I effectively manage them alongside this one?
9. Would it be advisable to consult with a specialist?
10. Are there any pamphlets or printed materials available that I can obtain?
11. Which websites do you suggest for additional information?

Asking these questions can foster open communication, align expectations, and contribute to a collaborative and productive therapeutic relationship.

What to Expect From Your Doctor

Your healthcare or mental health professional is likely to pose several inquiries. For instance:

- What symptoms are causing concern for you or your loved ones?
- When did you or your loved ones initially observe these symptoms?
- Are there periods in your life when you experience memory gaps?
- Have you ever found yourself at a considerable distance from your home or workplace, with no recollection of how you got there?
- Do you ever sense an experience of being outside your body, observing yourself?
- Do you perceive the presence of more than one person, or perhaps several individuals, coexisting within your mind?
- What other symptoms or behaviors are causing distress for you or your loved ones?
- How frequently do you experience feelings of anxiety or depression?
- Have your symptoms adversely affected your work or personal relationships?
- Have you ever contemplated self-harm or harming others?
- Do you engage in alcohol consumption or drug use?
- Are you presently serving or have you served in the military?
- Have you experienced any unwanted physical contact?

- Were you subjected to physical abuse or neglect during childhood?
- Was anyone in your family subjected to abuse during your childhood?
- Are you currently undergoing treatment for any other medical conditions, including mental health conditions?

Be prepared to respond to these inquiries to optimize your time for discussing the matters that are most pertinent to you.

EMDR is a psychotherapeutic technique that aids in processing traumatic experiences. It has demonstrated effectiveness in treating various trauma-related issues. However, its conventional use may not benefit all individuals with dissociative disorders. Therefore, it's crucial to customize the treatment for safety and efficacy. Adjustments to the basic EMDR protocol address unique needs associated with dissociative disorders, aiming to create a personalized, safe, and supportive environment for individuals navigating their traumatic experiences.

On the other hand, group therapy plays a limited but potentially valuable role in the treatment of dissociative disorders. While traditional group therapy may not be the primary mode of intervention, it can prove useful in specific instances where individuals with dissociative disorders can derive benefits from sharing their experiences with others who share similar conditions. The communal setting allows for a sense of understanding and connection, fostering a supportive environment where individuals can feel heard and validated. This can be particularly beneficial in addressing certain aspects of dissociative disorders and enhancing the overall therapeutic process.

What if Therapy Fails

When you find that therapy doesn't seem to be yielding the expected results, it's crucial to take proactive steps to reassess the situation.

The first step is to thoroughly re-evaluate the diagnosis and treatment plan to ensure that the technique chosen is appropriate for your individual needs. If your current therapist lacks experience in treating dissociative disorders, it might be beneficial to seek out a specialist with expertise in this specific area. The goal is to ensure that the treatment is tailored to your unique circumstances.

If traditional talk therapy proves ineffective, there are alternative avenues to explore. Consider incorporating alternative therapies like body movement therapy or mindfulness-based interventions, which may offer a different perspective and potentially lead to more effective outcomes. These alternatives can provide a fresh approach to addressing dissociative disorders, catering to your individual preferences and responses.

In certain situations, assembling a comprehensive treatment team may be necessary. This team could include clinicians, therapists, family therapists, and specialists in techniques like eye movement desensitization and reprocessing (EMDR). Collaborating with a diverse team of professionals allows for a more holistic and targeted approach to address the complexities of dissociative disorders.

It's essential to acknowledge that the road to recovery from dissociative disorders can be prolonged and challenging. Progress may unfold slowly, and setbacks are a natural part of the process. However, with the right treatment and support, you can navigate and manage your symptoms, ultimately enhancing your quality of life. Patience, persistence, and a collaborative approach with a supportive treatment team can significantly contribute to your journey toward improvement and well-being.

MEDICATION

Medication is a component of the treatment approach for dissociative disorders, although it's important to note that there are no psychiatric medications specifically designed to target the symptoms of dissociative disorders directly. Research, however, suggests that certain combinations of medications can effectively address dissociative conditions, particularly when they co-occur with other psychiatric disorders. By treating underlying conditions that contribute to dissociative symptoms, an improvement in dissociative conditions can be achieved.

- **Antidepressants**

Antidepressants are essential in the pharmacological management of dissociative disorders. Given that individuals with dissociative disorders frequently have concurrent psychiatric issues like depression and anxiety, it is crucial to address these comorbid conditions to effectively manage dissociative symptoms. Antidepressants, notably selective serotonin reuptake inhibitors (SSRIs) used alongside lamotrigine (an anticonvulsant and mood stabilizer), have demonstrated effectiveness in treating dissociative disorders, particularly depersonalization-derealization disorder. By stabilizing mood and alleviating intrusive symptoms, antidepressants contribute significantly to an overall improvement in the dissociative condition.

- **Antianxiety medications**

Antianxiety medications are another category of medications employed in the treatment of dissociative disorders. Anxiety and dissociation often co-occur, with each potentially exacerbating the other. Treating anxiety symptoms becomes crucial in reducing the severity of dissociative symptoms. Anxiolytic medications, which reduce hyperarousal and intrusive symptoms, can be effective in managing dissociative disorders. SSRIs, commonly used to treat anxiety, are also considered suitable for individuals with dissociative disorders. It's worth noting that benzodiazepines, typically used to manage anxiety, are usually contraindicated as they may exacerbate dissociation.

- **Antipsychotic medications**

Although dissociative disorders are not classified as psychotic disorders, antipsychotic medications can be incorporated into the treatment strategy. Atypical antipsychotic medications have demonstrated the ability to stabilize mood and alleviate anxiety and intrusive symptoms in individuals with dissociative disorders. Even though psychotic symptoms are uncommon in dissociative disorders, these medications can be advantageous in handling various non-psychotic psychiatric disorders linked to dissociative conditions. This comprehensive medication approach for treating dissociative disorders involves managing coexisting conditions and utilizing medications proven to be effective in stabilizing mood and mitigating intrusive symptoms.

In conclusion, creating a secure treatment environment is crucial for addressing dissociation, a coping mechanism developed in response to overwhelming emotions, particularly after traumatic experiences. While temporary dissociation can be adaptive, frequent and intense occurrences can impede concentration, learning, memory, and interpersonal connections. Treatment aims to establish a safe and relaxed setting to reduce dissociation and integrate mind functions. Psychotherapy, though lacking robust empirical evidence across various approaches, remains pivotal. Selecting an appropriate therapist, especially in complex cases necessitating a multidisciplinary treatment team, is paramount. Ultimately, the comprehensive approach to medication and therapy is tailored to your unique needs and aims to enhance your overall well-being. In the next chapters, we will explore strategies of how to overcome these dissociation disorders.

PART TWO
OVERCOMING WITH SELF-HELP STRATEGIES

CHAPTER 5

READYING A PERSONAL CRISIS PLAN

A personal mental health crisis is a situation wherein an individual displays behaviors posing a potential threat to themselves or others. To address such emergencies proactively, a mental health crisis plan is developed. This plan outlines the necessary steps to be taken in the event of a psychiatric emergency, where the individual may exhibit behaviors with potential harm. The purpose of the plan is to be prepared ahead of time, ensuring both the individual and their support network are aware of the appropriate actions to take during an emergency. Components of the plan can encompass details such as triggers, symptoms, procedures for seeking professional help, and indications for hospitalization or emergency services. Typically, this plan is collaboratively created with input from a mental health professional and the individual's support network. Having a pre-established crisis plan can significantly aid in effectively managing a mental health emergency and potentially prevent severe consequences.

WHY YOU NEED A PERSONAL CRISIS PLAN

Creating a personal crisis plan for dissociation is essential for several reasons, each addressing different aspects of your mental health and well-being:

- **Preparation for unexpected situations**

Developing a crisis plan is vital, as it empowers you to anticipate and manage unexpected situations that might trigger dissociation or exacerbate your symptoms. This forward-thinking strategy guarantees your readiness to navigate challenging circumstances promptly. By devising a comprehensive plan, you position yourself to quickly tap into the support and resources essential for effective coping. For instance, if certain stressors or triggers are identified in the plan, such as work-related pressure or social situations, you can proactively implement coping mechanisms or seek support from friends, family, or mental health professionals before the situation escalates. In essence, a well-crafted crisis plan serves as a personalized guide, enabling you to proactively address potential challenges and access the necessary assistance swiftly, ultimately contributing to better mental health management.

- **Reducing the risk of harm**

In situations where one grapples with persistent and severe suicidal thoughts, self-injurious behavior, or the potential for harming others, the presence of a crisis plan is crucial. This plan acts as a lifeline, offering a detailed roadmap to minimize risks and ensure safety. It is customized to individual needs, delineating specific safety measures and coping strategies. Consider it a personalized shield, providing protection against the hazards associated with such behaviors. During moments of crisis, the plan becomes a guiding light, furnishing clear directions on safely navigating through the darkness. Whether through reaching out to a trusted friend, employing coping mechanisms, or seeking professional assistance, the plan empowers individuals to take proactive steps towards their well-being, assuring that they are not alone in confronting these challenges.

- **Promoting self-care**

A personal crisis plan places a strong emphasis on self-care and self-compassion, recognizing their critical role in managing dissociation and its symptoms. By prioritizing your well-being, you empower yourself to better cope with dissociative episodes, ultimately reducing their frequency and severity. The plan becomes a tool for nurturing yourself during challenging times.

- **Supporting recovery**

Throughout your journey of recovery, the crisis plan plays a pivotal role beyond merely managing crises; it transforms into an essential roadmap that supports your overall healing process. It provides a structured approach for you to seek professional assistance, actively participate in therapeutic interventions, and engage with support groups. This comprehensive strategy empowers you to navigate the path to recovery with clarity and purpose. The plan not only addresses immediate crises but also establishes a framework for your long-term well-being. This personalized guide ensures that you have a systematic and proactive approach, fostering resilience and promoting sustained progress in your journey towards a healthier and more fulfilling life.

- **Strengthening your support network**

To enrich your support network, you actively incorporate ways to connect with individuals who have faced similar experiences, turning your crisis plan into a pathway to a nurturing community. By cultivating these connections, you establish a crucial space for sharing resources, exchanging knowledge, and finding emotional support. The collaborative nature of this plan significantly strengthens your coping mechanisms, giving you a sturdy foundation for overall well-being. Through shared experiences, you discover comfort and resilience, building bonds that ease the challenges of difficult times. Embracing this network enables you to navigate hardships with collective strength, offering not just a safety net during crises but also a continual source of support on your journey toward personal growth and recovery.

- **Encouraging a sense of control**

Creating a crisis plan instills a sense of control over your life and responses to dissociative episodes. As you construct this strategic roadmap, you gain a profound understanding of your triggers and responses, which leads to a proactive approach to symptom management. Your personalized plan becomes a tangible representation of your capability to take charge, which instills confidence in your ability to confront challenges directly. Recognizing your capacity to influence your experiences provides you with a powerful toolset, promoting resilience and diminishing feelings of helplessness. Ultimately, crafting a crisis plan becomes a self-affirming journey for you, reinforcing your agency in shaping your responses and life. This process contributes to cultivating a more confident and resilient mindset as you actively participate in the construction of strategies for managing difficult moments.

BUILDING A PERSONAL CRISIS PLAN

A mental health crisis plan is a proactive strategy developed in advance to guide actions in the event of an emergency, ensuring both you and your support system are well-prepared.

Crafting a crisis plan involves assembling a comprehensive list of resources, information, and instructions. This proactive approach is crucial, as decision-making and logical thinking often become challenging in times of extreme stress.

The primary purpose of a crisis plan is to ready oneself for potential mental health emergencies.

While you have the option to independently create your crisis plan, seeking assistance from a mental health professional or involving your support network can enhance its effectiveness.

Your crisis plan can be personalized for individual use, or you may choose to share it with your treatment team and loved ones. In some cases, there may be legal documents required, particularly for severe conditions.

Building a personal crisis plan is a crucial step in managing your mental health effectively. This plan is tailored to your unique needs and experiences, providing a structured approach to overcome challenging situations.

Identifying Triggers

Recognizing your triggers involves gaining insight into the specific events, situations, or conditions that could potentially negatively impact your well-being. These triggers are highly individualized, varying from person to person and encompassing factors like stressful situations, particular environments, or dynamics within certain relationships. For instance, tight work deadlines, crowded spaces, or conflicts in personal relationships might act as triggers for you. The power of identifying these triggers lies in your ability to foresee potential challenges. By understanding the circumstances that may contribute to a decline in your mental health, you empower yourself to take proactive steps and implement preventive measures. If, for example, you recognize that workplace pressure is a trigger, you can develop strategies like time management techniques or seeking support from colleagues to mitigate the impact on your mental well-being.

Crisis Manifestations

Crisis manifestations involve recognizing changes in your mood, behavior, or thought patterns. These manifestations serve as signals that you might be entering a mental health crisis. Observing alterations in how you feel, act, or think becomes crucial in understanding and addressing potential mental health challenges. Here are some examples of crisis manifestations that individuals might experience:

1. Changes in mood:

- increased irritability or agitation
- intense feelings of sadness or hopelessness
- heightened anxiety or panic attacks
- sudden mood swings or emotional instability

2. Changes in behavior:

- withdrawal from social interactions or activities once enjoyed
- increased use of substances (alcohol, drugs) as a coping mechanism
- restlessness or difficulty focusing on tasks
- engaging in risky behaviors or self-destructive actions

3. Changes in thought patterns:

- racing thoughts or inability to concentrate
- heightened paranoia or suspiciousness
- distorted perceptions of reality (hallucinations or delusions)
- intrusive or obsessive thoughts that are distressing

Recognizing these signs and symptoms requires self-awareness and an understanding of how they manifest uniquely in your own experience. For instance, you might notice that when you're on the brink of a crisis, your mood becomes increasingly erratic, your behavior becomes more impulsive, and your thoughts become more obsessive. Early detection of these warning indicators allows you to take proactive measures to manage your mental health, such as consulting a therapist or trusted friend, engaging in relaxation exercises, or following your personal crisis plan's crisis coping mechanisms. By being proactive, you can stop a problem from getting worse and advance general well-being.

Emergency Contacts

Maintaining a comprehensive list of emergency contacts is essential to ensure swift and effective support during challenging times. These contacts play a vital role in your personal crisis plan, serving as a network of individuals ready to offer assistance when required. The inclusion of various types of contacts, such as friends, family members, mental health professionals, or helplines, enhances the versatility of the support system.

For example, friends and family members can offer immediate emotional support and understanding, providing a sense of connection during a crisis. Mental health professionals, including therapists or counselors, bring expertise and guidance to navigate complex situations. Additionally, helplines, such as crisis hotlines, offer specialized assistance and resources specifically designed to address urgent mental health needs.

It is crucial to communicate with these individuals beforehand, ensuring they understand their role in your crisis plan. This clarity enhances the efficiency of the support network, as each contact becomes a reliable resource ready to provide the necessary aid when it is most needed. By proactively establishing and maintaining these connections, you strengthen the foundation of your mental health support system, promoting resilience and well-being during challenging times.

Crisis Coping Strategies

Crisis coping strategies consist of predetermined actions and coping mechanisms crafted to guide you through managing a mental health crisis. These encompass a variety of approaches that you can deploy when facing challenging circumstances. Examples of such strategies involve engaging in mindfulness exercises, practicing relaxation techniques, and participating in activities that have proven effective in enhancing mental well-being.

Essentially, when facing a crisis, the strategies you employ become like a toolbox, providing various options to tackle the specific aspects of the situation. For example, incorporating mindfulness techniques like meditation or deep breathing can aid in grounding and soothing your mind amidst intense stress. Taking part in activities that bring you comfort and happiness, like indulging in a beloved book or enjoying a stroll in nature, serves as a helpful diversion and supports your emotional health.

The key is to tailor these strategies to your individual preferences and needs, ensuring that you have a versatile array of tools at your disposal. By having a varied set of coping mechanisms, you can adapt and choose the most effective strategy based on the specific circumstances of the crisis, enhancing your ability to manage and mitigate its impact on your mental health.

Wellness Recovery Action Plan (WRAP)

The Wellness Recovery Action Plan is a comprehensive component that encompasses various aspects of maintaining mental well-being:

- **List of wellness tools:** This involves identifying and compiling a set of tools and activities that promote your mental health and well-being.
- **Daily routine:** Establishing a consistent daily routine helps provide structure and stability, contributing to overall mental wellness.
- **Your stressors:** Identifying sources of stress enables you to manage and minimize their impact on your mental health.

- **Early warning signs:** Recognizing early warning signs allows you to intervene before a crisis escalates.
- **Crisis plan:** Clearly outlining steps to take during a crisis, including accessing professional help if necessary.
- **Post-crisis plan:** Developing a plan for recovery and self-care after a crisis has occurred.

What should your mental health crisis plan include?

When creating a crisis plan, it's essential to reflect on past emergencies. Consider what unfolded during those times, identify the support you wished for but lacked, and determine the knowledge that could have been beneficial at that moment.

Your crisis plan is a personalized strategy, unique to you and your specific circumstances. It extends beyond just the plan itself; it also involves deciding whom you will share it with. It's vital that your partner is familiar with the crisis plan.

To structure your crisis plan effectively, the process is divided into two main components:

1. Medical information

Having this information readily available, even if not immediately needed in a crisis, can be invaluable for anyone, especially healthcare professionals like an emergency room doctor, who may not be familiar with your health history.

Here's an overview of the information to consider including in your crisis plan:

Basic Medical Information

- **Emergency contacts:** List individuals who should be contacted in case of an emergency.
- **Primary care doctor and mental health professionals:** Include names and contact information for your primary care physician, therapist, and psychiatrist.
- **Additional information:** Provide any other details that might be helpful, such as insurance information.

Medical History

- **Allergies or reactions to medications:** Document any known allergies or adverse reactions to medications.
- **Severe side effects of psychiatric medications:** Note any history of severe side effects related to psychiatric medications.
- **Past conditions, illnesses, or medical procedures:** Outline any significant past medical conditions, illnesses, or procedures.
- **Past psychiatric hospitalizations:** Specify if you have a history of psychiatric hospitalizations.

Current Medical Information

- **Current diagnoses:** List any current medical diagnoses you have.
- **Current medications:** Provide details about your current medications, including the date prescribed, the prescriber, and the dosage.
- **Other substances:** Include anything else you are currently taking, such as supplements or recreational drugs, to prevent potential interactions.

This comprehensive information ensures that healthcare professionals can make informed decisions about your care in a crisis, even if they are not familiar with your health history. It enhances the efficiency and effectiveness of emergency medical interventions and promotes better overall healthcare management.

2. Crisis plan

When formulating your crisis plan, consider incorporating the following:

- Contact information for psychiatric care facilities, your local mental health agency, and hotline numbers, among other emergency options.
- A step-by-step guide to getting expert help during a crisis.
- Recognizing the behaviors that point to the necessity of hospitalization.
- Identifying behaviors that necessitate a 911 call right away.

Remember, you don't have to create your crisis plan in isolation. Working with a mental health specialist can assist you with figuring out which behaviors to include and the best emergency resource numbers.

Ensure you have multiple copies of your plan and share them with your support team. Additionally, update the medical information whenever there are changes to your medication regimen. This organized approach enhances the effectiveness of your crisis plan, ensuring you and your support network are well-prepared for mental health emergencies.

Crisis Plan Template

Personalized Crisis Plan

Your name:

____

Emergency contacts:

1. *Name:* _______________________
Relationship: _______________________
Phone number: _______________________

2. *Name:* _______________________
Relationship: _______________________
Phone number: _______________________

3. *Name:* _______________________
Relationship: _______________________
Phone number: _______________________

Emergency resource numbers:

- *Hotline:* _______________________
- *Local mental health department:* _______________________
- *Psychiatric care center:* _______________________

Steps to follow if you need professional help:

1. *First step:* _______________________
2. *Second step:* _______________________
3. *Third step:* _______________________

Behaviors indicating hospitalization:

- *Behavior 1:* _______________________
- *Behavior 2:* _______________________
- *Behavior 3:* _______________________

Behaviors indicating 911 call:

- *Behavior 1:* _______________________
- *Behavior 2:* _______________________
- *Behavior 3:* _______________________

Pro tip:

For easy access to your emergency resource, save the main number as *Crisis* in your phone book.

Additional notes:

____

____

____

Share this plan with your support team and ensure you have multiple copies. Regularly update medical information, especially when there are changes to your medication.

Remember, this crisis plan is a personalized tool to guide you and your support network during challenging times. Regularly review and adjust it as needed to ensure its relevance to your current mental health needs.

In conclusion, understanding and addressing personal crises in mental health is crucial. A well-prepared crisis plan is a proactive strategy to navigate psychiatric emergencies effectively. By incorporating elements such as identifying triggers, emergency contacts, and coping strategies, you not only enhance your ability to manage crises but also promote self-care, strengthen your support network, and encourage a sense of control. Building a comprehensive mental health crisis plan is an empowering step towards recovery and well-being. In the next chapter, we will learn about the practical strategies for managing dissociation.

CHAPTER 6
PRACTICAL STRATEGIES

Dealing with dissociation involves practical approaches to minimize its effects. When you experience dissociation, you can employ grounding exercises to reconnect with the present moment and your surroundings. These exercises often involve sensory activities like deep breathing, touching different objects for tactile sensations, or vividly describing the environment.

To further manage dissociation, it's crucial to establish a safe and calming environment. This includes identifying and eliminating triggers, which maintains a consistent routine, and has a reliable support system in place.

Moreover, psychotherapy techniques, such as cognitive behavioral therapy, dialectical behavioral therapy, and psychodynamic therapy, can be valuable in addressing dissociation and its underlying causes. These therapeutic interventions provide a structured framework to understand and manage dissociative experiences.

In general, practical strategies like grounding exercises, creating a safe environment, and seeking appropriate therapeutic interventions play a key role in helping individuals cope with dissociation and lessen its negative impact on their lives.

PRACTICAL STRATEGIES FOR MANAGING DISSOCIATION

Self-Monitoring for Dissociation

Self-monitoring is a technique where individuals track and record their own behavior, providing detailed information about various aspects such as the time spent, the context of occurrence, the specific form of behavior, and the emotions experienced during its performance. This method is particularly employed when individuals are working towards changing or controlling their behavior.

For instance, a therapist might assign self-monitoring as homework to a client with the intention of promoting better self-regulation. By consistently documenting their actions and related details, individuals gain insight into patterns, triggers, and emotions associated with their behavior. This awareness becomes a valuable tool in the process of behavior modification, helping individuals make informed decisions and work towards positive change. Essentially, self-monitoring serves as a reflective and empowering practice that enhances an individual's ability to manage and adapt their behavior in a more intentional and constructive manner.

Self-monitoring is a fundamental component of cognitive-behavioral therapy (CBT). The process involves two main elements: discrimination and recording.

Discrimination

Discrimination refers to the process of identifying and being aware of specific target phenomena, which, in this case, are the symptoms, thoughts, and emotions experienced by clients. For many clients, this task can be challenging, as it might be the first time they are actively paying attention to and acknowledging their own mental and emotional experiences.

Clients may express concerns about doing this self-awareness exercise correctly. To make it more accessible, therapists can simplify the process. One approach is to ask clients to simply note whether the target phenomena are present or absent, without delving into detailed descriptions. Another strategy involves varying the questions therapists use to explore these thoughts and feelings. Instead of focusing on complex thoughts or mental images, therapists might instruct clients to monitor more noticeable body sensations or observable behaviors.

Essentially, the goal is to help clients build awareness of their internal experiences without overwhelming them. Simplifying the process and providing alternative ways to approach the exercise can make it more manageable and less intimidating for clients who may be new to exploring their symptoms, thoughts, and emotions in therapy.

Recording

Recording, in therapy, is the crucial act of noting events and experiences. Clients use this method to monitor thoughts, feelings, and behaviors. It involves documenting occurrences, like anxiety, detailing when it happened, duration, circumstances, and activities. This structured approach enables clients to self-monitor, identifying patterns, triggers, and gaining insights into emotional influences. Reviewing recorded experiences over time helps analyze patterns, identify commonalities, and make informed decisions about mental health management. Overall, recording is a powerful tool for self-awareness, reflection, and empowerment in therapeutic processes, facilitating an active role in mental health management.

Self-monitoring can be achieved through various tools, each serving a specific purpose:

- **Diaries**

Diaries are effective for recording the timing of events in your life, such as daily activities, sleep patterns, or instances of pain. They provide a chronological account of your experiences, helping you identify patterns and correlations between different aspects of your life and well-being.

- **Logs**

Logs are useful for tracking the frequency of events, behaviors, thoughts, or emotions. They allow you to quantify occurrences over time, providing a quantitative perspective on your experiences. For example, you can use logs to document how often a particular behavior or emotion occurs, helping you gain insights into your habits and triggers.

- **Records**

Records serve as a tool for documenting detailed information about your thoughts, memories, symptoms, or responses to various situations. Unlike simple logs, records offer a more in-depth exploration of your internal experiences. They can be valuable for capturing nuanced details, facilitating a better understanding of the factors influencing your mental and emotional well-being.

Why Practice Self-Monitoring

- **Enhance your performance**

Utilizing self-monitoring can elevate your work performance by pinpointing your strengths and weaknesses, establishing achievable goals, and monitoring your progress. Awareness of your emotions and stress levels enables you to adapt strategies, enhancing your ability to cope with challenges. For instance, recognizing pre-presentation anxiety allows you to employ relaxation techniques or seek feedback. Additionally, self-monitoring fosters acknowledgment and celebration of achievements, fostering motivation and confidence.

- **Effectively manage your emotions**

Self-monitoring aids in the effective management of emotions by identifying triggers, understanding their impact, and facilitating appropriate expression. Awareness of emotions prevents interference with decision-making, problem-solving, and communication. For example, if post-conflict anger arises, taking a break, calming oneself, and considering the other person's perspective becomes possible. Developing emotional intelligence, encompassing empathy and adept communication, is an additional benefit of self-monitoring.

- **Improve interpersonal relationships**

Self-monitoring contributes to enhanced relationships by adapting behavior and communication style to diverse situations and individuals. Awareness of one's impression on others helps avoid misunderstandings, conflicts, and negative perceptions. Adjusting participation levels in a meeting based on self-awareness is an illustrative example. Building trust, rapport, and collaboration with colleagues, managers, and clients is another positive outcome of effective self-monitoring.

- **Practicing self-monitoring**

Developing self-monitoring as a skill involves maintaining a journal or log documenting emotions, thoughts, and behaviors across various situations. Regularly reviewing this log provides insights into strengths, weaknesses, and areas for improvement. Seeking constructive feedback from others offers valuable external perspectives. Experimenting with diverse strategies and techniques for emotional management and performance improvement is crucial. Overall, self-monitoring emerges as a powerful tool for personal growth, facilitating success in both career and life, and enhancing overall happiness and satisfaction.

Types of Self-Monitoring

They include:

- **Acquisitive self-monitoring**

Acquisitive self-monitoring refers to an individual's tendency to be highly attuned to external cues and social expectations in order to acquire and assimilate information about their surroundings.

Individuals with a high acquisitive self-monitoring orientation are adept at adjusting their behavior and expressions to fit various social contexts. They are observant of social norms, quick to recognize and adapt to social expectations, and often skilled at presenting themselves in ways that align with the expectations of different social settings. Acquisitive self-monitors are typically effective in navigating diverse social environments, and may excel in situations that require adaptability and social dexterity. However, there is a risk of adapting too much and sacrificing authenticity for social approval.

- **Protective self-monitoring**

Protective self-monitoring involves a heightened awareness of one's behavior, expressions, and personal information with the goal of safeguarding oneself from potential risks or negative outcomes. Individuals with a protective self-monitoring orientation are cautious about revealing too much about themselves and are selective in the information they share. This type of self-monitoring is driven by a desire to manage impressions and avoid vulnerability. Protective self-monitors may be strategic in their interactions, carefully considering the potential consequences of their words and actions. While this approach can be beneficial in certain situations, it may also lead to guarded or reserved behavior, making it challenging for others to truly understand the individual on a deeper level.

How to Conduct Self-Monitoring for Dissociation

Self-monitoring for dissociation involves systematically tracking and analyzing various aspects of your experiences to gain insights into patterns, triggers, and coping strategies. Here's a guide on conducting self-monitoring using a six-step template:

- **Step 1: Choosing a focus, purpose, and prompt for data collection**: Determine the specific aspect of dissociation you want to monitor, such as triggers, frequency, or severity. Ensure that the purpose is to clarify your goal for self-monitoring, whether it's increasing awareness, identifying triggers, or evaluating coping strategies. Then define a cue or reminder to initiate data collection, ensuring consistency and reliability in your monitoring process.
- **Step 2: Situation**: Note down the details of the situation or context in which the dissociative episode occurred. These details may include the location, time of day, activities engaged in, and people present during the episode.
- **Step 3: Dissociation**: Document the onset, duration, intensity, and specific dissociative symptoms experienced. Describe feelings of detachment, loss of time, depersonalization, derealization, or identity confusion.
- **Step 4: Thoughts**: Write down any thoughts or cognitive patterns associated with the dissociative episode. Record thoughts of disconnection, unreality, confusion, or fear during the experience.
- **Step 5: Emotions and body feelings:** Recognize and document the emotions and physical sensations accompanying dissociation. Record feelings of anxiety, numbness, emptiness, or tingling sensations in the body.
- **Step 6: Responses**: Reflect on the responses or coping strategies employed during or after the dissociative episode. Document efforts to ground yourself, seek support from others, practice relaxation techniques, or engage in self-care activities.

Alter Check-Ins

1. Personal information

My name: _______________________________

My age: _________

My gender: __________

2. Introduce yourself

(Share a brief description of who you are, your personality, and any other information you feel comfortable sharing.)

3. My hopes for the future

(Outline your aspirations and goals for the future, whether they're personal, professional, or related to specific life experiences.)

4. Role

(Describe your current role or roles in life, such as work, student, caregiver, etc.)

5. Positive trigger

(Identify activities, situations, or experiences that positively influence your mood or well-being.)

6. My sexuality

(Share your sexual orientation or any details you feel comfortable expressing about your sexuality.)

7. My dislikes

(List things, activities, or situations that you dislike or find challenging.)

8. Hobbies
(List activities or hobbies that bring you joy and fulfillment, helping you unwind or express yourself creatively.)

9. Negative triggers
(Identify situations, words, or actions that may act as triggers for negative emotions or experiences.)

Closing thoughts: Anything else you'd like to share
(Provide an open space for any additional information or thoughts you would like to share.)

Logging Dissociation Worksheet

Date: _______________________

Time started: _____________________

Duration: __________ minutes

Situation details

Location:

____

People present:

____

____

Activities engaged in:

____

____

Dissociation observations

Onset:

____

Duration:

____

Intensity (Scale 1-10):

____

Specific symptoms experienced

- Detachment:
- Loss of time:
- Depersonalization:
- Derealization:
- Identity confusion:

Thoughts during dissociation

____

Emotions and body feelings

Emotions:

____

____

____

Physical sensations:

____

____

Responses and coping strategies

Efforts to ground yourself:

____

Seeking support:

____

Practicing relaxation techniques:

____

Engaging in self-care activities:

____

After the episode:

Reflections:

____

____

____

Additional notes

____

____

____

This worksheet is designed for personal reflection. Fill in the details as honestly and comprehensively as possible. Use this tool to track your experiences and gain insights into patterns and triggers related to dissociation.

Relaxation Techniques

Relaxation techniques are strategies employed to alleviate stress and promote a sense of calmness in both mind and body. They play a crucial role in managing dissociation by helping individuals regain control over their thoughts and emotions. Here are two common relaxation techniques:

- **Grounding techniques**

Grounding techniques are designed to anchor you in the present moment, fostering a stronger connection to reality and reducing feelings of detachment from your surroundings. By actively engaging your five senses, these techniques bring your attention to the here and now. For instance, you might count objects in the room, walk barefoot on the grass, hold an ice cube, or wrap yourself in a comforting blanket—all of which can effectively ground you. These exercises help you interrupt dissociative episodes, allowing you to refocus on sensory experiences and reestablish a sense of presence and stability in your surroundings.

Some of the grounding techniques mentioned here will be discussed in more detail in the following chapter, providing additional tools and strategies for managing dissociation.

- **Physical activity**

Participating in physical activities like exercise, dancing, or stretching can serve as a potent means to lessen dissociation. When you engage actively in aerobic exercises like jogging, dancing, or cycling, you're not merely enhancing your physical fitness; you're also exerting a positive influence on your mental health. Research indicates that these activities can effectively alleviate sensations of anxiety and depression, resulting in an overall enhancement of your mood and cognitive abilities.

As you integrate physical activity into your daily routine, you'll likely notice a rise in your self-esteem. Achieving fitness milestones and prioritizing your physical health can lead to a more positive view of yourself. Moreover, engaging in movement-based activities offers chances for social interaction. This not only combats feelings of loneliness but also builds relationships with others, which is especially advantageous for those managing dissociative disorders. By actively participating in physical activities, you're not only boosting your overall well-being but also opening doors to enhanced self-esteem and social bonding.

Mindfulness

Mindfulness is a powerful technique that can assist you in managing dissociation by fostering a heightened awareness of your present experiences. It's important to recognize that while mindfulness exercises can be beneficial, they are not a cure-all, and seeking professional help from a therapist is crucial for comprehensive support.

- **Mindfulness of the external world**

To enhance your capacity to turn towards reality with openness and curiosity, especially in severe dissociative states, begin by mindfully exploring the external world. Engage your senses: What do you see, hear, touch, taste, and smell? Practice mindfulness with activities like observing sounds in the room, drinking a glass of water with full awareness, looking out the window with focused attention, feeling the texture of your jacket mindfully, smelling a flower with intention, or taking a walk outside to consciously experience everything around you. This process helps you gradually reconnect with reality and build resilience against experiential avoidance, fostering a more grounded and present state of mind.

- **Mindfulness of the body-world juncture**

Engaging in mindfulness at the intersection of your body and the external world is a valuable practice. Instead of delving into internal thoughts and emotions, focus on your body's connection with the surroundings. For instance, you can ground yourself by pressing your feet into the floor, actively feeling the contact. Another technique involves tactile awareness, such as touching the chair beneath you or feeling the texture of your clothing. By directing attention to these physical sensations, you create a present-moment awareness that helps in reducing dissociation and fostering a connection with your immediate environment.

- **Mindfulness of body's surface**

When you feel emotionally numb inside, pay attention to surface-level changes in your body: tears on your face, warmth in your cheeks, tingling or coldness in your fingers, or sweaty palms. Mindfully observe these physical cues; they can serve as entry points to reconnect with your emotions. For instance, notice the movement of your ribcage during deep breaths or the warmth spreading across your face when expressing emotion. By acknowledging these sensations, you can begin the process of reconnecting with your internal emotional experiences.

- **Turning away, turning towards**

For those experiencing dissociation, redirecting attention from distressing emotions to neutral physical sensations can be helpful. Instead of avoiding feelings, you can actively engage in harmless activities like stretching. Try stretching your arms and feel the muscles tensing in your forearms, upper arms, and shoulders. Push your feet into the floor, noticing the tension in your thigh muscles. By turning towards these physical sensations, you create a mindful connection with your body, promoting a grounded and present experience.

- **Posture and movement**

In improving self-awareness, practicing mindfulness in observing your body posture and movements proves beneficial. Experiment by sitting both slouched and upright, or with legs crossed and uncrossed, paying attention to the effects on your mindset. Additionally, engage in various movements like stretching, walking, or rubbing hands together, observing them mindfully. This self-exploration enhances your understanding of how body dynamics impact your mental state, contributing to overall well-being.

- **Mindful breathing**

Mindful breathing may vary in effectiveness for clients; some find it beneficial, while others may dislike or feel anxious about breath-focused exercises. You can focus on the external world, notice changes in your body's "surface," be aware of your posture and movement, or engage in mindfulness of strong yet harmless physical sensations, like controlled muscle stretching or tensing and releasing.

- **Graded exposure**

When you consciously face challenging thoughts and emotions, expanding your psychological flexibility, it's called "interoceptive exposure." Engaging in "graded exposure," you gradually confront less challenging stimuli before advancing to more intense ones. For instance, if public speaking triggers anxiety, you might start by visualizing a small audience before progressing to speaking in front of larger groups. This intentional approach allows you to navigate discomfort systematically, fostering resilience and adaptability.

- **Values guided exposure**

In Acceptance and Commitment Therapy (ACT), values-guided exposure involves facing challenging thoughts and feelings aligned with one's values for a richer life. Instead of merely exposing clients to distressing stimuli, the focus is on helping them live authentically. If you, as the client, can't see the link between facing difficult emotions and creating a more fulfilling life, resistance may arise. The "pushing away paper exercise" is a powerful tool in ACT, illustrating the transformative connection between facing fears and embracing a meaningful existence. The "pushing away paper exercise" is a cognitive strategy where individuals physically distance themselves from written materials or documents to temporarily detach from stressors or overwhelming information. By physically pushing aside the papers, it symbolizes a mental break and a deliberate effort to create space from the challenges at hand. This exercise is often used as a simple yet effective technique to manage stress and regain mental clarity.

- **The feared inner world**

As you become more skilled in mindfully observing less confronting aspects of reality, the next step involves facing more challenging elements—your thoughts, feelings, emotions, and memories that you may typically avoid. If you tend to "go numb," a beneficial progression is ultra-quick body scans. You can start with brief 30-second scans, gradually increasing the duration. As your mindfulness skills advance, consider extending scans to 20 or 30 minutes. If you only sense numbness, mindfully acknowledge it, or try creating sensations by stretching or contracting muscles.

- **Naming feelings**

Recognize and name your emotions deliberately, heightening your conscious awareness of the diverse feelings you're undergoing. This practice involves accurately identifying and labeling your emotional state, fostering self-awareness and contributing to emotional regulation. Acknowledging and naming emotions is a key step in understanding and managing one's internal experiences.

- **Dropping anchor**

Dropping anchor is a mindfulness technique to combat dissociation, offering a metaphorical tether to the present. Imagine fixating on a cherished item, like a calming pebble, or repeating a comforting mantra when you feel detached. This chosen anchor becomes a steadfast reference point, steadying you amidst dissociative moments. Much like a ship anchored in a storm, this intentional focus provides stability, helping you regain connection with the present and navigate through challenging emotions with a sense of grounding and security.

Cognitive Restructuring

In your journey to manage dissociation, cognitive restructuring stands as a pivotal element in Cognitive-Behavioral Therapy (CBT). This process actively involves challenging and transforming dysfunctional beliefs and perceptions that contribute to dissociative experiences. Within the cognitive-behavioral model, clinical interventions aimed at reducing dissociation encompass reality testing, decisional balance, Socratic questioning, emotion regulation, attentional training, and mindfulness-based programs. By incorporating these strategies, you can actively participate in reshaping thought patterns and perceptions, ultimately promoting a more grounded and connected experience.

For those navigating post-traumatic stress disorder (PTSD), dissociation is recognized as an ineffective coping strategy. Here, you may find yourself holding dysfunctional beliefs about dissociation. Cognitive therapy emerges as a valuable tool, effectively assisting you in forming a practical conceptualization of dissociative symptoms linked to trauma. This process encourages understanding and active management of dissociative experiences within the context of PTSD.

If you're grappling with derealization, a form of dissociation triggered by factors like chronic stress, trauma, or mental health disorders, cognitive restructuring becomes a beneficial approach. By engaging in this process, you can explore and transform dysfunctional beliefs, fostering a more connected and grounded experience in the face of derealization.

Furthermore, studies have unveiled a significant association between dissociation and obsessive-compulsive disorder (OCD). As part of cognitive-behavioral therapy for OCD, cognitive restructuring plays a vital role. This approach empowers you to challenge and reshape thought patterns, contributing to a more effective and comprehensive strategy in managing the complex interplay of dissociation within the context of OCD.

Socratic Questioning Worksheet for Dissociation

Date: _______________________

Time started: _________________________

1. Identifying dysfunctional thoughts

What thought or belief triggered your dissociation episode?
How would you describe this thought or belief?

____

2. Challenging beliefs

Are there alternative ways to view this situation that might be less distressing?
What evidence supports or contradicts your initial thought or belief?

____

3. Exploring assumptions

What assumptions are you making about yourself, others, or the situation?

How might someone else view this situation differently?

---

4. Considering consequences

What are the potential consequences of continuing to believe in this thought?

What might be the consequences if you let go of or challenge this thought?

---

5. Testing reality

What objective evidence do you have for and against this thought?

If a friend had a similar thought, what would you tell them?

---

6. Developing balanced thoughts

What is a more balanced and realistic thought to replace the initial one?

How does adopting this new thought impact your feelings and behaviors?

---

7. Reflection

How do you feel now compared to when you started this exercise?

What did you learn about the thought patterns contributing to your dissociation?

This Socratic questioning worksheet is designed to guide you through the process of challenging and reframing thoughts associated with dissociation. Use it regularly to enhance your self-awareness and develop a more adaptive perspective on your experiences.

Decisional Balance Exercise for Dissociation

Instructions

The decisional balance exercise is intended to help you consider the benefits and drawbacks of controlling your dissociation disorder. Take your time reflecting on each of the following aspects. Be honest with yourself, and think about how each factor affects your life.

Pros of managing dissociation disorder

1. Improved daily functioning
2. Better relationships with others
3. Increased sense of control
4. Enhanced self-awareness
5. Greater emotional stability

Cons of managing dissociation disorder

1. Time and effort required for therapy or self-care activities
2. Possible discomfort or emotional distress during treatment
3. Fear of facing traumatic memories or experiences
4. Initial challenges in implementing coping strategies
5. Potential resistance from others or societal stigma

Reflection

Consider the following questions and write down your thoughts:

- What are the most significant pros of managing your dissociation disorder for you personally?

- What are the main barriers or challenges you anticipate in managing your dissociation disorder?
- How do the pros outweigh the cons, or vice versa, in your decision to actively address your dissociation disorder?

Action plan

Based on your reflections, outline concrete steps you can take to address your dissociation disorder. Consider seeking professional help, practicing self-care techniques, or reaching out to supportive friends or family members.

1. ______________________________________
2. ______________________________________
3. ______________________________________
4. ______________________________________
5. ______________________________________

Final thoughts

Remember that managing dissociation disorder is a journey, and it's okay to seek support along the way. Celebrate your progress, no matter how small, and be gentle with yourself during challenging moments.

Emotional Regulation Worksheet

Date: ______________

1. Grounding techniques

- Choose at least two grounding techniques from the list below to practice when you feel dissociation coming on:

- deep breathing
- five senses check (list five things you can see, hear, touch, smell, and taste)
- holding onto a comfort object
- progressive muscle relaxation

2. Identifying triggers

- List potential triggers for your dissociation episodes:

  - ______________________________
  - ______________________________
  - ______________________________

3. Emotional check-in

- Rate your current emotional state on a scale of 1 to 10 (1 being calm, 10 being highly distressed):
- Your emotion: ______________________
- Intensity level: ______________________

4. Thought records

- Write down any negative thoughts or beliefs you're currently experiencing. Challenge and reframe them if possible.
- Negative thought: ______________________
- Challenge/reframe: ______________________

5. Self-compassion

- List three kind and compassionate things you can say to yourself in this moment:

  - ○ ______________________________
  - ○ ______________________________
  - ○ ______________________________

6. Coping strategies

- Identify healthy coping strategies you can engage in right now:

  - ○ ______________________________
  - ○ ______________________________
  - ○ ______________________________

7. Post-reflection

- After practicing the above techniques, reflect on how you feel now compared to when you started.

____

____

____

Note: This worksheet is a tool for self-reflection and management of dissociation symptoms. It is recommended to seek professional support for a more comprehensive and tailored approach to dissociative disorders.

Self-compassion

Developing self-awareness, self-esteem, and self-compassion is a fundamental basis for overcoming the challenges linked with dissociation, providing the tools to lead a more enriching life. Developing a significant understanding of your thoughts, emotions, and triggers equips you to navigate the intricacies of dissociation with heightened clarity. Building self-esteem entails acknowledging your strengths and accomplishments, reinforcing resilience against the impact of dissociative experiences. Moreover, embracing self-compassion allows for a kind and supportive inner dialogue during difficult moments. This comprehensive approach to self-growth establishes a sturdy foundation, empowering you to confront and triumph over the hurdles presented by dissociation, ultimately paving the path to a more gratifying and purposeful existence.

Enhancing your self-compassion skills is vital for your well-being. Here are five actionable ways to give yourself a quick self-compassion boost:

- **Comfort your body**

Nurture yourself physically. Eat something nutritious, rest, or indulge in self-massage, focusing on areas like your neck, feet, or hands. Even a simple walk can significantly improve your physical well-being, providing an instant dose of self-compassion.

- **Write a letter to yourself**

Reflect on a challenging situation without blame, whether it's a breakup, job loss, or a difficult presentation. Draft a letter to yourself, acknowledging the pain without assigning fault. This exercise serves as a nurturing outlet for your emotions.

- **Give yourself encouragement**

Imagine what supportive words you'd offer a dear friend facing a tough situation. When you encounter challenges, channel these compassionate responses toward yourself. Extend the same kindness and encouragement you would to a friend.

- **Practice mindfulness**

Incorporate mindfulness into your routine, even if briefly. A few minutes of meditation can foster self-acceptance during challenging times, promoting a sense of nurturing and understanding towards yourself.

- **Journal**

Keep a dedicated journal focused on examining instances of self-criticism. Record the circumstances, thoughts, and emotions linked to moments when you are overly harsh on yourself. Employ this journaling method as a means of self-reflection, aiding in the recognition of recurring patterns. Through this practice, foster the ability to develop a progressively more compassionate outlook over time.

By incorporating these practices into your life, you actively cultivate self-compassion, fostering a more resilient and supportive relationship with yourself.

Creating Structure and Routine

Creating structure and routine in your everyday life provides various psychological benefits that contribute to overall well-being:

- **Reduced stress:** Planning provides a sense of control, minimizing stress. Having predetermined decisions allows you to focus on making quality choices for those that remain.
- **Improved sleep:** A consistent sleep schedule enhances rest. Establishing a bedtime routine aids in falling asleep faster, contributing to better overall sleep quality and a positive psychological impact.
- **Enhanced health:** Meal planning facilitates a healthy diet, requiring dedicated time for shopping and preparation. A routine can also support regular physical activity and timely medication intake, fostering a healthier body and mind.
- **Increased happiness:** Scheduling allows for dedicated playtime, crucial for adult mental health. Whether reading, gaming, or enjoying nature, planned downtime contributes to overall happiness, preventing the day's end without moments of pleasure.

Create Your Routine

Creating Your Healthy Routine Worksheet

Utilize this worksheet to assist you in crafting a customized and health-conscious routine. Regularly evaluate and modify your schedule to align with changing needs and aspirations.

Personal information

- **Name:** ______________
- **Date:** ______________
- **Current daily schedule: (if applicable)**

____

1. Define your priorities

- List your top three priorities in life (e.g., health, work, relationships).

____

____

____

2. Set realistic goals

- Identify short-term and long-term goals related to your priorities.

____

____

____

3. Morning routine

Design a morning routine that aligns with your priorities and goals.

wake-up time:

activities (e.g., meditation, exercise, breakfast):

____

____

____

____

____

____

4. Daytime schedule

Outline your typical activities and commitments during the day.

work/study hours: ___________________
breaks:

____

____

meals:

____

____

____

5. Evening routine

Create an evening routine to wind down and prepare for the next day.

dinner time: _____________________
relaxation activities (e.g., reading, stretching):

____

____

____

sleep time: _____________________

6. Self-care practices

List activities that contribute to your well-being.

physical exercise: _____________________
mental health practices (e.g., mindfulness, journaling):

____

____

leisure activities:

____

____

____

7. Flexibility and adaptability

Plan for flexibility in your routine to accommodate unexpected events.

> How will you adjust your routine during busy or challenging days?

____

____

____

8. Reflection

Reflect on your routine and its alignment with your goals.

> What adjustments might enhance your routine for better well-being?

____

____

____

> How can you ensure a balance between productivity and self-care?

____

____

____

9. Implementation plan

Break down your routine into actionable steps.

> What will you implement first?

____

____

____

How will you track your progress?

____

____

____

10. Commitment pledge:

Write a commitment statement to solidify your dedication to the new routine.

____

____

____

____

____

____

Time Management

Your mental health is significantly impacted by how well you manage your time. Efficient time management empowers you to fulfill responsibilities, decrease stress, and boost overall life satisfaction. When you organize your schedule effectively, you ensure that you allocate time for work, self-care, and leisure, facilitating the maintenance of a healthy balance in your life.

Prioritizing tasks and establishing achievable goals empowers you to cultivate a sense of accomplishment and regain control over your life. This practice fosters a positive mindset and diminishes feelings of being overwhelmed. Effective time management, tailored to your needs, additionally promotes improved sleep hygiene. Structured routines contribute to regulating sleep patterns, thereby positively influencing your mental and emotional resilience. Embracing these habits allows you to take charge of your daily experiences, enhancing your overall well-being and empowering you to navigate life with a greater sense of balance and fulfillment.

Write It Down

Time Management and Stress Reduction Worksheet

Personal information

Name: _________________

Date: _________________

1. Prioritize your tasks

List your top three priorities for the day or week. Consider both work and personal responsibilities.

2. Set Realistic goals

Establish achievable short-term and long-term goals related to your priorities.

3. Create a daily schedule

Outline a typical day, including work/study hours, breaks, meals, and leisure activities.

4. Time blocking

Allocate specific blocks of time for different tasks to enhance focus and efficiency.

5. Identify time-wasting habits

List any habits or activities that consume time without significant benefits. Consider ways to minimize or eliminate them.

6. Break down tasks

Divide larger tasks into smaller, more manageable steps. This helps prevent feeling overwhelmed.

7. Delegate responsibilities

Identify tasks that can be delegated to others, either at work or in your personal life.

8. Set boundaries

Establish clear boundaries for work, social media, and other potential distractions to maintain focus.

9. Plan regular breaks

Schedule short breaks throughout the day to prevent burnout and improve overall productivity.

10. Reflect and adjust

Regularly assess your time management strategies. What is working well, and where can you make improvements?

11. Stress-reducing activities

List activities that help alleviate stress. Incorporate them into your schedule for self-care.

12. Create a relaxing evening routine

Develop a routine to wind down before bedtime, promoting better sleep quality.

13. Commitment pledge:

Write a commitment statement to follow through with your time management plan.

As you conclude this chapter, you've embarked on a journey exploring practical strategies for managing dissociation. Addressing **you** directly, the chapter talks about relaxation techniques, emphasizing the efficacy of slow breathing, grounding methods, and physical activity in alleviating dissociation symptoms. It explores the transformative power of mindfulness and cognitive restructuring, providing resources and practical exercises. The chapter culminates with self-compassion insights, offering you tools to develop resilience, create routines, manage time effectively, and enhance your overall well-being. In the next chapter, you will learn the significance of grounding techniques for managing dissociation.

CHAPTER 7

GROUNDING TECHNIQUES

As discussed before, dissociation is a defense mechanism your body adopts to shield you from intense emotions and distress, especially after trauma. This coping strategy creates a mental detachment. When you experience dissociation, you can employ grounding exercises, which aid you in reestablishing a connection with the present and your environment. These exercises guide you back to reality, offering a way to manage overwhelming feelings and navigate through difficult experiences.

GROUNDING TECHNIQUES

Grounding is the practice of connecting with the present moment and anchoring yourself in reality. It involves focusing on your senses and surroundings to maintain a sense of stability and balance. Essentially, it's like planting your feet firmly on the ground, both metaphorically and physically, to stay rooted in the current experience.

Grounding is important because it allows you to remain anchored amid challenges and uncertainties. Being present and fully aware of your surroundings provides a mental and emotional foundation that might save you from feeling overwhelmed or disoriented. This technique might be especially effective when you're stressed, anxious, or have racing thoughts. Grounding techniques are a practical and efficient approach to return your focus back to the present moment, providing a sense of control and calm. In essence, grounding is a useful skill for sustaining your well-being and dealing with life's ups and downs more resiliently.

Preparing for Using the Grounding Techniques for Dissociation

When you experience dissociation, it's usually a response to feeling unsafe or overwhelmed. To effectively manage dissociation using grounding techniques, it's important to recognize and understand your triggers, as well as the bodily cues that indicate you've been triggered.

- **Start by identifying your triggers.** This means paying attention to situations, memories, or emotions that provoke a dissociative response. For example, if crowded spaces make you feel anxious due to past experiences, that could be a trigger. Recognizing these triggers helps you connect the current situation with past events, bringing you back to the present moment. It may require reflection and possibly guidance from a therapist to uncover and understand these triggers fully.
- **Notice the cues that you've been triggered.** These cues vary from person to person and can include physical sensations like a dry mouth, tension, sweating, or racing thoughts. For instance, if you notice your heart racing and your palms getting sweaty during a stressful conversation,

it could be a cue that you're starting to dissociate. By becoming aware of these bodily signals, you can intervene more effectively. The more you practice recognizing these cues, the better you'll become at responding to them promptly and reorienting yourself to the present moment.

How Grounding Techniques Work

Grounding techniques function by reconnecting you with your body, countering the fear associated with dissociation—the unsettling feeling of detachment from oneself. The deeper the disconnection, the more anxiety tends to escalate. Given that attempting to think your way into a sense of safety is ineffective, grounding techniques serve as practical tools to facilitate reconnection with yourself and the present moment. In order to make the grounding techniques work effectively, you can follow the following steps.

- **Step 1: Noticing your triggers**

Start observing the lead-up to your dissociative states, noting thoughts, context, and events. By curiously and non-judgmentally examining these aspects, you can identify triggers.

- **Step 2: Noticing your bodily cues**

Pay attention to physical signals, such as clumsiness, sweating, rapid heartbeat, concentration difficulties, or an unreal feeling. Consistently observe these cues leading up to dissociative episodes. Acknowledging triggers and bodily cues may require practice, especially if you've been accustomed to disconnecting from your body.

- **Step 3: Using your body's cues to intervene**

Once you've developed self-observation skills, you can recognize certain cues as warning signs indicating an upcoming dissociative state. Your objective is to intervene when these signals emerge, halting the dissociation process effectively. This stage underscores the significance of fostering awareness through activities such as mindfulness, yoga, or meditation. Engaging in these practices enhances your capacity to identify and react to bodily signals, ultimately aiding in the prevention of dissociative episodes.

Sensory Grounding

Sensory grounding involves using your senses to connect with the present moment and create a sense of stability. The five, four, three, two, one grounding technique is a method that utilizes your senses to achieve this. Here's a detailed explanation:

1. **Five things you can see:** Take a moment to observe and identify five things around you. It could be the color of the walls, objects on your desk, or anything in your immediate environment. This helps redirect your focus to the visual stimuli in your surroundings.
2. **Four things you can touch:** Pay attention to the sense of touch by identifying four things you can physically feel. It might be the texture of your clothing, the warmth of a cup in your hand, or the surface you're sitting on. This tactile awareness helps ground you in the present.
3. **Three things you can hear:** Take note of three unique sounds in your area. It could be the buzz of a computer, the rustle of leaves, or distant road noise. Engaging with aural stimuli helps to direct your attention to the noises around you.

4. **Two things you can smell:** Focus on your sense of smell by identifying two scents in your surroundings. It might be the aroma of coffee, a scented candle, or even natural outdoor scents. This olfactory awareness helps anchor you in the present moment.

5. **One thing you can taste:** Lastly, pay attention to your sense of taste. Identify one thing you can taste, whether it's a lingering flavor from a recent meal, a sip of a drink, or chewing gum. This gustatory focus brings your attention to the present through the sense of taste.

Cognitive Grounding

Cognitive grounding involves employing various techniques to anchor your thoughts in the present moment and promote mental stability. Here are some methods for cognitive grounding:

- **Name things in a category:** Categorization involves actively stimulating your mind by naming things within a specific category. For instance, create a list of various fruits or animals and look into the details of each item. By doing so, you challenge your cognitive processes, redirecting your thoughts away from stressors. This mental exercise not only promotes concentration but also introduces an element of playfulness, making it an effective technique for grounding your mind in the present.

- **Use affirmations:** Affirmations serve as powerful tools to reshape your thought patterns and establish a positive mindset. Craft personalized affirmations that resonate with your goals and values. Repeating these affirmations helps reinforce a constructive narrative, counteracting negative thoughts. By consciously focusing on optimistic statements, you can cultivate a more resilient and empowered mindset, creating a mental environment conducive to overall well-being.

- **Describe your surroundings:** Descriptive awareness anchors you in the present by encouraging a detailed exploration of your surroundings. Pay close attention to colors, textures, and sounds, fostering a heightened sense of mindfulness. This practice connects you to the current environment, creating a buffer against intrusive thoughts. Descriptive awareness serves as a practical and immediate grounding technique, promoting a conscious connection to the richness of the present moment.
- **Practice mindfulness meditation:** Mindfulness meditation involves purposeful activities that improve your awareness and concentration. You can participate in this method by focusing on your breath, sensations, or a particular focal point. By nurturing a non-judgmental awareness of your thoughts, mindfulness lowers stress levels and enhances mental clarity for you. Consistent practice enhances your capacity to remain in the present moment, equipping you with essential skills to handle stressors and sustain a stable mental equilibrium.

Emotional Grounding

Emotional grounding involves utilizing various techniques to manage and navigate strong negative emotions effectively. Here are some methods to help you with emotional grounding:

- **Let your emotions flow:** Embrace your emotions without judgment. If you're feeling sadness, let yourself experience it without pushing it away. Acknowledge the emotion's presence, identify it, and recognize where it manifests physically. For example, if you're angry, notice the tension in your shoulders. Allow the emotion to circulate naturally through your awareness, fostering a deeper understanding of your emotional landscape.

- **Breathe the emotion down to your feet:** Visualize a calming release for negative emotions. Inhale deeply, imagining your breath drawing in the emotion like a magnet. As you exhale, picture the emotion flowing down through your body and out through your feet, being absorbed by the earth. For instance, if you're feeling anxiety, visualize the tension leaving your body with each exhale. Repeat this visualization until you feel a tangible sense of calm and lightness.

- **Inhale "here", exhale "now":** Develop mindfulness by practicing focused breathing. Begin by closing your eyes and inhaling deeply while mentally acknowledging "here," then exhaling while acknowledging "now." Improve your concentration by placing your hand on your belly, noticing its movement with each breath. If distractions occur, gently guide your attention back to your breathing. This straightforward activity assists you in staying grounded in the present moment, fostering mental clarity.

- **Notice your body's contact with the floor or chair:** Connect with your physical surroundings to ground yourself during emotional moments. Pay attention to the sensation of the chair against your back or the floor under your feet. To engage more actively, "grab" the floor with your toes or feel the texture of your socks. This tactile awareness provides a tangible connection to the present, fostering stability as you navigate your emotions.

- **Pay attention to your belly:** Use your breath and physical touch to center yourself. Place your hands on your belly, observing the rise and fall with each breath. This deep-breathing technique serves as a reliable anchor during overwhelming emotions. For example, if you're feeling stress, focus on the rhythmic expansion and contraction of your belly, allowing it to guide you back to a calmer state.

VISUALIZATION TECHNIQUES

Utilizing visualization proves beneficial for individuals experiencing dissociative disorders to alleviate symptoms. This technique entails forming a mental image of a secure and soothing environment, fostering a sense of grounding and presence. It is crucial to recognize that incorporating guided imagery may not always be without challenges, particularly regarding timing and persuasion.

To enhance effectiveness and mitigate potential issues, it is advisable to integrate visualization with other grounding methods like breathing exercises and sensory awareness. This holistic approach ensures a more comprehensive strategy, aiding individuals in maintaining a connection to the present moment and effectively managing dissociative symptoms.

Guided Imagery

Guided imagery is a therapeutic technique where a person, often a guide or therapist, verbally leads individuals through a detailed script to evoke mental images and sensations. It's a powerful tool that can be particularly helpful for managing dissociation, a psychological experience where individuals may feel detached from their thoughts, feelings, or surroundings.

Let's have a three-minute exploration to guide you through powerful imagery techniques designed to help you navigate and overcome moments of dissociation. Find a comfortable space and take a deep breath as we dive into the realm of your imagination.

[Minute 1: Grounding in nature]

Close your eyes and imagine a serene forest. Feel the soft earth beneath your feet, the rustling leaves overhead. With each breath, visualize roots extending from your body into the ground, grounding you in the present moment. This connection with nature serves as a foundation, bringing you back to reality.

[Minute 2: Balancing elements]

Picture yourself near a calming body of water—a gentle stream or a tranquil lake. As you breathe, imagine inhaling the soothing qualities of water, bringing balance and clarity to your mind. Feel the warmth of the sun on your skin, absorbing its energizing rays. Envision these elements harmonizing within you, restoring equilibrium.

[Minute 3: Safe haven visualization]

Now, envision a safe and comforting space—a haven that's uniquely yours. It could be a cozy room, a favorite spot, or even a peaceful beach. Take a moment to explore this place, engaging all your senses. Notice the colors, textures, and sounds around you. This space is your sanctuary, a retreat where you are entirely present and secure.

As you open your eyes, carry the tranquility of this journey with you. Remember, these guided imagery techniques are your tools to combat dissociation. Anytime you feel disconnected, revisit this mental sanctuary. You're equipped to face any dissociative moment with strength and resilience.

Safe Place Visualization

Safe place visualization is a therapeutic technique where you mentally construct and immerse yourself in a comforting, secure haven. This personal sanctuary is designed to evoke feelings of safety, tranquility, and well-being. By vividly imagining and engaging with this imagined space, individuals can find emotional relief, reduce stress, and enhance resilience. It serves as a psychological retreat, fostering a sense of calm that can be accessed at any time to promote mental health and cope with challenges.

In this three-minute guided imagery session for managing dissociation, find a quiet and comfortable space to relax. Close your eyes, take a deep breath, and imagine a serene sanctuary. Visualize yourself in a safe place, surrounded by tranquility. Picture the details— the gentle rustle of leaves, the soothing warmth of sunlight, or the calming sound of ocean waves.

As you breathe deeply, focus on the sensations of safety and peace enveloping you. Visualize a protective cocoon, shielding you from any distressing thoughts or emotions. You are in control of this safe space, and it is here to provide comfort.

Now, bring attention to your body. Feel the steadiness of the ground beneath you, grounding you in the present moment. Imagine a soft, supportive light surrounding you, dispelling any disconnection you may feel. Envision this light restoring a sense of unity within yourself.

As you continue to breathe, acknowledge any sensations or emotions with compassion. Remind yourself that you are safe in this moment. Embrace the comforting atmosphere, and when you're ready, gently open your eyes, carrying this sense of safety with you into the world.

Remember, this safe place visualization is a tool always available to you, helping you navigate moments of dissociation with a renewed connection to the present and a feeling of security.

Future Self Visualization

Future self visualization is a mental exercise where you imagine and vividly picture your ideal future. By visualizing your future self, you create a detailed mental image of your aspirations, achievements, and desired lifestyle. This technique helps motivate and guide present actions, fostering a sense of purpose and direction. It allows individuals to connect with their goals on a deeper level, inspiring confidence and commitment to personal growth and success.

To practice this technique, sit or lie down comfortably, taking a deep breath in and exhaling slowly. Imagine a serene garden. Visualize yourself walking through this garden, feeling the softness of the grass beneath your feet. As you explore, notice the vibrant colors of flowers around you. Each flower represents a positive aspect of yourself.

Now, imagine a warm, gentle light enveloping you, bringing a sense of calm and security. Allow this light to gradually fill the garden, dispelling any shadows or negative thoughts. As the light surrounds you, affirm to yourself that you are safe and grounded.

In the next moments, visualize a protective shield forming around you. This shield acts as a barrier against dissociation. Picture it as a strong, resilient force keeping you connected to the present moment. Feel the reassurance that, with this shield, you have the power to stay anchored and engaged in your surroundings.

As you conclude this imagery session, take another deep breath and open your eyes. Carry the sense of grounding and protection with you throughout your day, knowing that you have the ability to navigate challenges with resilience and presence.

In this chapter, you've explored vital grounding techniques for managing dissociation. Understanding its essence and significance for well-being, you've equipped yourself with personalized steps, recognizing triggers and cues. Discover the transformative power of sensory, cognitive, and emotional grounding methods with detailed resources. Immersed in therapeutic visualization techniques like guided imagery, safe place, and future self-visualization, you now possess practical tools to empower yourself and navigate dissociation's challenges. In the next chapter, you will discover the pivotal role supportive relationships play in your journey with dissociative disorders.

CHAPTER 8

BUILDING YOUR SUPPORT SYSTEM

In my relationship with my partner, we have had a challenging journey as she struggles with dissociation. Despite her dedication to therapy and psychiatric support, engaging in serious conversations has proven to be a formidable task. Whenever we disagree on any issue, attempting to find common ground becomes challenging, often disrupted by her tendency to dissociate.

The frustration is palpable. It's not about blaming her; I understand her struggle. Yet, my attempts at honesty, seeking compromise, or solving problems are met with a disheartening silence. In those moments, she stares into emptiness, repeating a tic-like motion with her hand until the episode concludes. Despite my efforts, nothing gets resolved, leaving both of us in a lingering state of distress.

In response, I extend love and support, seeking to ground her and ensure her well-being. However, my gestures are met with resistance; she retreats, desiring no connection during these episodes. It's a challenging journey, one where love and understanding grapple with the complexities of mental health, which leaves me torn between the desire for resolution and the need to navigate her dissociative struggles.

ROLE OF SUPPORTIVE RELATIONSHIPS

Supportive relationships are extremely important in your recovery from dissociative disorders. You are not alone in this struggle, and the support, understanding, and empathy provided by others around you can aid in your healing. You require a network of individuals who actively listen to your experiences without passing judgment, creating a secure space for you to communicate your thoughts and emotions. These relationships can help you feel acknowledged and understood, establishing a sense of belonging and decreasing the isolation that often comes with dissociative disorders.

Supportive relationships act as an important anchor, grounding you in reality and helping to counteract the detachment that defines dissociation. During difficult times, these connections bring stability and comfort by delivering practical assistance as well as emotional support. With a strong support system, you are better able to traverse the difficulties of therapy and self-discovery, resulting in a more comprehensive and long-lasting recovery. Finally, the function of supportive connections goes beyond ordinary companionship; they act as pillars of strength, helping you to fight and conquer the obstacles of dissociative illnesses.

You may be familiar with the concept of inpatient care, but have you ever explored the benefits of Intensive Outpatient Programs (IOP)? In contrast to receiving care within a residential facility, Intensive IOP provides a well-organized level of support, enabling individuals to adhere to their regular daily schedules. IOP often occurs within group settings, which leads to a supportive atmosphere wherein individuals can interact with peers who have comparable experiences and face similar challenges. In an IOP, you have the opportunity to receive comprehensive therapeutic interventions, counseling, and support while still being actively involved in your community and daily life. This unique approach fosters a sense of connection and understanding among participants, enhancing the overall effectiveness of the treatment and promoting a smoother transition back to everyday life.

HOW TO BUILD SUPPORTIVE RELATIONSHIPS

Building supportive relationships while managing dissociative disorders requires many critical measures that can significantly improve your overall well-being:

- **Invest time**

Devoting time to fostering individual connections proves vital for both personal development and the fortification of your relationships. Initiate meaningful conversations, actively listen, and genuinely show interest in the lives of others. Through these actions, you establish a foundation for trust and understanding, nurturing a more profound connection with the people in your life.

- **Communicate effectively**

Effective communication is a skill that you should actively develop. Prioritize openness, honesty, and professionalism in your interactions. Develop the art of active listening, demonstrating your ability to focus on what others are saying without passing judgment. Through clear and transparent communication, you contribute to the establishment of trust, a foundational element in supportive relationships.

- **Respect and appreciate others**

Respecting and appreciating others, regardless of their role, is crucial for building strong connections. Acknowledge the value of diverse opinions and ideas, creating an inclusive environment that not only strengthens your relationships but also enhances mutual respect within them. By valuing the unique perspectives of those around you, you contribute to a more enriching and supportive social network.

- **Set and respect boundaries**

Establishing and honoring boundaries constitutes a vital element in sustaining positive relationships. It is imperative to articulate your needs and expectations clearly, while acknowledging and respecting the limits set by others. This practice guarantees a harmonious and mutually respectful engagement, fostering a sustainable and constructive connection in both your personal and professional spheres.

- **Work collaboratively**

Foster collaboration by actively participating in shared endeavors. Be willing to contribute ideas, work together, and offer support. Collaborative efforts can strengthen the bonds between individuals, providing a solid foundation for a supportive relationship.

- **Let go of control**

Understand that trying to control others can be detrimental to relationships. Trust others to fulfill their responsibilities and contribute to the relationship. Letting go of control promotes a more balanced and harmonious connection.

- **Reflect and learn**

Reflect on past relationships to gain insights into what worked well and what didn't. Use this self-awareness to continuously learn and grow, adapting your approach to improve future relationships.

- **Be positive**

Cultivate a positive attitude in your interactions. Focus on the positive aspects of others, offering support and encouragement. A positive outlook contributes significantly to the creation and maintenance of healthy, supportive relationships.

GIVING THE SUPPORT THEY NEED

Supporting someone experiencing dissociation involves actively engaging in their journey to recovery. Here are the different ways you can help them:

- **Educate yourself**

You should take the initiative to educate yourself about dissociation and its symptoms. Understanding the nature of dissociation will equip you to comprehend what your loved one is going through. This acquired knowledge facilitates a more empathetic approach, enabling you to identify signs accurately and offer appropriate support effectively.

- **Offer support and understanding**

Be patient and understanding. You need to acknowledge that dissociation can be triggered by various factors. It's crucial that you express your support and assure your loved one that you're there for them. Your willingness to listen without judgment and to validate their experiences creates a safe space for them to share their feelings.

- **Communicate openly**

Encourage open and honest communication. Let your loved one know that you are ready to listen to their experiences, feelings, and needs without judgment. By fostering a climate of open communication, you help them feel comfortable discussing their struggles, which is a crucial step in their journey toward healing.

- **Help them find professional help**

Assist them in researching and accessing appropriate therapy or treatment options. You can play a pivotal role by helping them navigate the often complex process of finding professional help. Offer to accompany them to appointments, help with research, or assist in making initial contact with healthcare professionals.

- **Encourage self-care**

Support them in engaging in activities that promote relaxation and well-being. Encourage practices such as slow breathing, grounding exercises, and physical activity. By actively joining them in their self-care rituals or proposing comforting activities, you play a role in fostering their general well-being and emphasizing the significance of self-care in their recovery.

- **Assist with daily life**

Provide assistance with everyday chores to alleviate stress. Contribute by helping with tasks like grocery shopping, cooking, or running errands. By shouldering these daily responsibilities, you enable your loved one to concentrate on their recovery without the additional burden of routine tasks.

- **Develop a crisis plan**

Collaborate with them to create a plan for managing dissociative episodes and coping with triggers. Work together to establish a detailed crisis plan that outlines specific strategies to navigate difficult moments. By involving them in the process, you ensure that the plan is tailored to their needs and preferences, making it a more effective tool for managing crises.

- **Promote safety and trust**

Encourage the open sharing of feelings and needs actively, collaborating to establish a secure and trustworthy environment. Your role as a dependable and empathetic presence actively contributes to creating a feeling of safety crucial for individuals undergoing dissociation. Your dedication to upholding trust nurtures a supportive connection that plays a vital role in their journey towards healing.

SELF-HELP RESOURCES

- **Mind.org**

You can turn to Mind.org for practical suggestions to help you cope with dissociation. This resource not only provides valuable information on managing dissociative experiences but also guides you on accessing treatment and support. The insights offered by Mind.org aim to empower you in navigating through the challenges associated with dissociation.

- **Psychology tools**

If you're looking for resources tailored to working with dissociation, Psychology Tools is here to assist you. This platform offers various tools, including audio collections and self-monitoring records, designed to aid you in understanding and addressing dissociative experiences. These resources are crafted to support your journey toward better mental well-being.

- **The survivors trust**

The Survivors Trust equips you with a dissociation toolkit and valuable resources. If you are dealing with dissociation, this platform is a reliable source for information on triggers and staying safe during dissociative episodes. It serves as a comprehensive guide, providing you with practical tools to manage and cope with dissociative challenges.

- **Online communities**

You do not have to face dissociation alone. There are various online communities where you can connect with people who have had similar experiences. These groups provide emotional support, understanding, and practical counsel as you navigate the challenges of dissociation. Notable platforms include:

- **The dissociative initiative:** This public network shares resources and information about dissociation, multiplicity, and amnesia from various perspectives. It's a space where you can connect with a diverse community to gain insights and support.
- **Discussing dissociation:** This forum encourages open and honest conversations about the layers of dissociative life. By connecting with others on a social level and within their inner systems, you'll find support and encouragement for living with dissociative disorders.
- **My support forums:** Specifically designed for individuals with dissociative disorders like DID, this emotional support group and friendship forum offer a safe space for sharing experiences and supporting each other through the unique challenges of dissociation.
- **ISSTD regional online communities:** The International Society for the Study of Trauma and Dissociation provides regional online communities that aim to enhance understanding of complex trauma and dissociation. Joining these communities can broaden your perspectives and knowledge.
- **PODS (Positive Outcomes for Dissociative Survivors):** As a charity promoting recovery from dissociative conditions, PODS shares research, resources, and information on dissociation. Engaging with this

community can be a positive step towards your journey of recovery, providing you with the necessary tools and support.

- **HeyPeers:** It thrives as a compassionate community featuring certified Peer Supporters. When you become a member, you have the opportunity to offer essential support to individuals in search of guidance and empathy from those who have traversed similar paths.
- **Meetup.com:** Operates as a social media platform dedicated to hosting and coordinating both in-person and virtual activities, gatherings, and events. It caters to people and communities sharing common interests, hobbies, and professions.

HOW YOU CAN SUPPORT YOUR FRIEND WITH DID

The fact is that there is no single action that guarantees this situation will never occur again. You don't need to strive for perfection in your role as a friend, attempting to avoid triggering statements or excessively worrying about excluding others. It's impossible to fully understand their thoughts, and the pursuit of absolute understanding is unattainable. There will inevitably be numerous aspects that remain unknown or misunderstood.

However, what you are capable of doing is:

- When supporting a friend, actively listen without expressing disinterest, as this can harm your relationship. Engage empathetically to create a safe space for them to share without fear.
- Respond with empathy and respect when someone shares their identity. Use proper pronouns and names to show acknowledgment and acceptance, positively impacting

their well-being and contributing to an inclusive environment.

- In moments of cognitive or emotional shifts, be patient and understanding. Allow your friend the time needed to process and adjust. If confusion arises, offer a brief recap or guide the conversation back to a comfortable topic, showcasing compassion and reinforcing trust in your friendship.

In conclusion, you've explored the crucial role of supportive relationships in the journey of individuals with dissociative disorders. By delving into the intricacies of building connections, understanding, and employing practical strategies, you've gained insights into effective communication and crisis planning. With a wealth of self-help resources and online communities, this chapter serves as a comprehensive guide for both you and your support networks.

APPENDIX I: FAQS

Here are some FAQs related to DID, focusing on questions that may not have been covered in other chapters:

How is DID different from schizophrenia?

Dissociative Identity Disorder (DID) and schizophrenia represent separate psychiatric conditions. In DID, you may experience the coexistence of two or more distinct identity states, each interacting with the world in its own way. Conversely, schizophrenia is mainly defined by disruptions in your thought processes, perceptions, and emotions. If you have schizophrenia, you might encounter hallucinations, delusions, and challenges in cognitive functioning. Despite both disorders involving changes in perception and consciousness, the underlying mechanisms and symptoms vary. It's important to recognize that these conditions differ in how they manifest, which emphasizes the uniqueness of each individual's mental health challenges.

Can someone with DID integrate all their identities into one?

Integration is a therapeutic goal in treating DID, but not everyone with DID achieves full integration. Integration involves merging separate identity states into a cohesive sense of self. However, the process is highly individualized, and some individuals may choose not to integrate fully, preferring instead to establish effective communication and cooperation among their identities. Therapy often focuses on improving the individual's overall functioning, well-being, and the ability to manage and navigate their internal experiences.

Are there cultural differences in the presentation of DID?

Research suggests that the prevalence and expression of DID may vary across cultures. Some cultures may have different conceptualizations of dissociation and may express these experiences in unique ways. Additionally, cultural factors influence how individuals and communities perceive and respond to mental health issues, affecting the diagnosis and treatment of DID. Culturally sensitive assessments and interventions are crucial to understanding and addressing DID in diverse populations.

How does DID manifest in children, and can it be mistaken for an active imagination?

DID can manifest in childhood, and it may be initially mistaken for an active imagination or other behavioral issues. Children with DID may exhibit sudden shifts in behavior, mood, or abilities. Memory gaps may be observed, and the child may struggle with integrating various aspects of their identity. It is essential for clinicians to conduct specialized assessments for children, considering factors such as play therapy and age-appropriate diagnostic tools, to accurately diagnose and address DID in this population.

What role do neurobiological factors play in the development of DID?

DID may involve neurobiological factors, encompassing changes in brain structure and function. Neuroimaging research has indicated variations in the brains of those with DID, particularly in regions linked to memory and identity. The connection between neurobiology and DID remains a subject of continual investigation, and it's probable that a blend of genetic, environmental, and neurobiological elements plays a role in the disorder's development. As you look into the understanding of DID, recognizing the complexity of its neurobiological underpinnings can shed light on the multifaceted factors contributing to its manifestation.

Is it possible to fake or simulate DID symptoms?

Faking DID is challenging due to the complexity and subtleties of the disorder. Mental health professionals employ rigorous diagnostic criteria and specialized assessments, such as structured clinical interviews and standardized measures, to differentiate between genuine DID and feigned symptoms. The comprehensive evaluation typically includes an exploration of the individual's life history, experiences of trauma, and an understanding of dissociative symptoms, making it difficult for someone to convincingly simulate the disorder.

How does treatment for DID differ from other dissociative disorders?

Treatment for DID involves a phased and individualized approach. It often begins with establishing safety and stabilization, addressing symptoms such as self-harm or substance abuse. Building trust between the individual and their therapist is crucial. Identity integration, where applicable, becomes a focus in later stages of therapy. While some aspects of treatment may overlap with other dissociative disorders, the emphasis on working with distinct identity states sets DID treatment apart. Therapeutic modalities commonly used include psychoeducation, cognitive-behavioral therapy, dialectical behavior therapy, and specialized approaches like internal family systems therapy. The goal is to improve overall functioning and enhance the individual's ability to cope with life's challenges.

Are there any advancements in neuroimaging techniques for studying DID?

Ongoing neuroimaging studies in DID are leveraging advancements in technologies such as functional magnetic resonance imaging (fMRI) and positron emission tomography (PET). These techniques allow researchers to look into the neural processes associated with DID. For instance, fMRI helps identify patterns of brain activation associated with different identity states, shedding light on the neurobiological underpinnings of the disorder. As technology evolves, researchers aim to refine their understanding of the neural correlates of DID, potentially paving the way for more targeted therapeutic interventions.

How does society perceive and stigmatize individuals with DID?

The varied societal perspectives on DID often stem from a lack of understanding, which leads to diverse opinions. Stigma arises when media depictions perpetuate misconceptions, sensationalizing, or distorting the nature of the disorder. It is vital to combat this stigma to promote understanding and solidarity. Initiatives such as public education campaigns, truthful media portrayals, and the sharing of personal experiences play key roles in dispelling stereotypes and diminishing the stigma linked to DID. Fostering open dialogues about mental health contributes to building a more inclusive and empathetic society.

Can individuals with DID lead productive and fulfilling lives?

Attaining a gratifying and effective life is possible for individuals with DID through appropriate treatment and assistance. The essential approach involves addressing the disorder's specific challenges, such as integrating identities and managing dissociative experiences. Therapeutic approaches like cognitive-behavioral therapy and dialectical behavior therapy focus on bolstering coping skills and improving daily functioning. By adhering to a comprehensive treatment strategy within a supportive environment, you can progress toward your personal and professional goals, ultimately contributing positively to society.

What is the role of family and social support in the treatment of DID?

Your journey with DID is significantly influenced by the support you receive from family and friends. Involving your family in the therapeutic process is crucial, as it fosters a more understanding and supportive environment for your healing. Educating them about DID enhances their capacity to offer effective support tailored to your needs. Additionally, the acceptance and connections you cultivate with friends and peers play a vital role in your recovery. It's essential for you to build a strong support network, as it will help you navigate the challenges associated with DID and contribute to your overall well-being.

How do therapists work with different identity states during therapy sessions?

To effectively address different identity states in individuals with DID, therapists use diverse therapeutic approaches like internal family systems therapy. These involve recognizing and comprehending the unique roles and functions of each identity, promoting communication, and fostering cooperation among them. You and your therapist collaborate to address trauma, improve coping mechanisms, and, when appropriate, facilitate integration. Building trust and ensuring safety in the therapeutic relationship is crucial for navigating the complexities of working with diverse identity states.

Is DID a lifelong condition, or can it be completely cured?

The course of DID varies among individuals, and complete "cure" is not always guaranteed. While some individuals may experience significant improvement and integration of identity states through therapy, others may manage the disorder over time. The focus of treatment is often on achieving substantial recovery and improving the individual's quality of life. Long-term therapy, ongoing support, and personalized strategies contribute to the individual's ability to lead a fulfilling life, even if complete eradication of all symptoms may not be achievable for everyone.

How do cultural and religious beliefs influence the perception and treatment of DID?

Cultural and religious beliefs significantly impact how individuals perceive and cope with DID. In some cultures, dissociative experiences may be viewed through a different lens, affecting the interpretation and acceptance of the disorder. Religious beliefs may influence coping strategies, with some individuals seeking support within their faith communities. Culturally sensitive approaches to treatment are essential, acknowledging and respecting diverse belief systems. Integrating cultural competence into therapy helps ensure that treatment aligns with an individual's cultural and religious context, fostering a more effective and respectful therapeutic relationship.

Can DID coexist with other mental health conditions?

If you have DID, it's common to face additional mental health issues simultaneously. This implies that alongside DID, you may also be dealing with other challenges like depression, anxiety, or post-traumatic stress disorder (PTSD). It's vital to undergo a thorough assessment to grasp the entirety of your mental health. The interplay between these coexisting conditions may impact each other, necessitating personalized treatment strategies. Attending to these comorbidities not only improves the success of therapeutic interventions but also contributes to your overall well-being.

How can individuals with DID advocate for themselves and reduce stigma?

Empowering individuals with DID to advocate for themselves involves sharing their stories, educating others, and actively participating in mental health awareness initiatives. By openly discussing their experiences, individuals with DID contribute to reducing stigma surrounding the disorder. Advocacy efforts can include participating in community events, engaging with mental health organizations, and leveraging social media platforms to amplify their voices. Through these efforts, individuals with DID play a crucial role in fostering understanding, compassion, and destigmatization within communities.

What are the ethical considerations in researching and studying DID?

Ethical considerations in DID research are paramount. Researchers must prioritize the well-being of participants by obtaining informed consent, ensuring confidentiality, and minimizing potential harm. Given the sensitive nature of DID, protecting identities becomes crucial to prevent inadvertent disclosure. Additionally, researchers must consider the potential for retraumatization and implement safeguards to mitigate this risk. Ethical research practices are fundamental to advancing knowledge responsibly and respecting the rights and dignity of individuals with DID.

How do gender and identity intersectionality impact the experience of DID?

Exploring the intersectionality of gender and identity in the context of DID is an emerging area of research. Gender identity can influence the manifestation and expression of dissociative symptoms. Understanding the unique challenges faced by individuals with DID who belong to diverse gender and identity groups is essential for providing inclusive and culturally competent care. Therapists should be attuned to these intersectional aspects, recognizing that experiences of identity and gender may intersect with and shape the lived experiences of individuals with DID.

Can trauma-informed care benefit individuals with DID even if they don't have a trauma history?

For someone with DID, trauma-informed care holds significance regardless of whether there's a documented trauma history. It revolves around establishing a secure and encouraging setting, recognizing the potential effects of trauma, and guaranteeing that your care is considerate and adaptable to your needs. Even if there's uncertainty about a particular trauma history, trauma-informed care promotes a therapeutic alliance founded on trust and sensitivity. It acknowledges that you may have undergone distressing events that you might not easily remember or share, highlighting the necessity of building a secure and affirming therapeutic space for you.

How do emerging therapeutic modalities, such as virtual reality, impact the treatment of DID?

Exploring the use of emerging therapeutic modalities, like virtual reality (VR), in the treatment of DID reflects an evolving approach to therapy. VR can provide controlled and immersive environments, allowing individuals to confront and process traumatic memories in a gradual and supportive manner. Therapists can use VR to simulate scenarios that help individuals navigate challenges associated with DID, such as identity integration. While still in the early stages of exploration, VR holds promise as a complementary tool that may enhance traditional therapeutic approaches for individuals with DID.

Can creative therapies, such as art or music therapy, be effective in treating DID?

Creative therapies, such as art and music therapy, exhibit potential in aiding individuals with DID. They provide alternative means of expression when verbal communication may pose challenges for you. Art and music therapy create avenues for you to look into and merge different facets of your identities, articulate emotions, and heighten self-awareness. By including creative therapies in your treatment plan, it can complement conventional therapeutic methods, presenting a comprehensive and individualized approach to cater to your distinct needs as someone with DID.

How does the legal system accommodate individuals with DID, particularly in legal proceedings?

Addressing the legal implications of DID is crucial, especially in legal proceedings where memory inconsistencies may pose challenges. Legal professionals must be educated on the nature of DID to ensure fair and just treatment. Accommodations may include allowing support persons during legal proceedings, taking into account the potential impact of dissociative symptoms on testimony reliability, and providing resources for mental health assessments to inform legal decisions. Sensitivity to the unique challenges faced by individuals with DID within the legal system is essential to uphold principles of fairness and justice.

Are there preventative measures or interventions for individuals at risk of developing DID?

While direct prevention of DID may not be possible, early intervention after trauma and the provision of mental health support are crucial in mitigating the risk of severe dissociative symptoms. Creating trauma-informed environments involves recognizing the prevalence and impact of trauma and ensuring that individuals receive appropriate support. This may include psychoeducation, counseling, and therapeutic interventions aimed at processing traumatic experiences. By addressing trauma promptly and offering support, the likelihood of dissociative disorders developing can be reduced.

What impact does DID have on the physical health of individuals?

Experiencing DID can greatly impact your physical health because of the ongoing stress linked to the disorder. Juggling various identity states, memories, and traumatic experiences can increase your body's physiological reactions. You might find yourself facing psychosomatic symptoms like headaches, gastrointestinal problems, and chronic pain. Sleep disruptions are typical, leaving you feeling tired and affecting your overall health negatively. It's crucial to include considerations for your physical health in your treatment plan. Working together with healthcare experts and mental health professionals ensures a comprehensive approach that tackles both the psychological and physical dimensions of your well-being.

How does DID affect the concept of self and identity in the digital age?

In the digital age, individuals with DID face unique challenges and opportunities in managing and expressing their identities online. Social media and digital platforms provide spaces for self-expression, but the presence of multiple identities within a single individual may complicate online interactions. Privacy concerns and the need to manage multiple digital identities require careful navigation. Therapists working with individuals with DID may play a role in helping clients establish healthy online identities, set boundaries, and manage the potential risks associated with online self-disclosure. Exploring these challenges contributes to a more comprehensive understanding of identity in the digital age.

What are the potential societal and economic costs associated with untreated or poorly managed DID?

Untreated or poorly managed DID can lead to significant societal and economic costs. Individuals facing challenges in education, employment, and relationships may become dependent on social services. The economic impact includes costs related to healthcare utilization, social support systems, and potential productivity losses in the workforce. Addressing DID through effective mental health interventions and support systems not only benefits individuals but also contributes to broader societal well-being and economic productivity. Investing in early intervention and appropriate treatment can mitigate long-term societal and economic burdens.

What are the ethical considerations in researching and studying DID?

Ethical considerations in DID research are multifaceted and require a delicate balance. Researchers must prioritize participant welfare by obtaining informed consent, maintaining confidentiality, and minimizing harm. Given the vulnerability of individuals with DID, ethical research practices involve transparent communication, ensuring that participants fully understand the nature and purpose of the study. Researchers must be cautious about potential retraumatization and should strive to contribute positively to the understanding and treatment of DID. Additionally, fostering a collaborative and respectful relationship between researchers and participants is essential to uphold the rights and dignity of those involved in the research.

How do gender and identity intersectionality impact the experience of DID?

When considering the intersectionality of gender and identity, it's important to understand how this complexity impacts the experience of DID. Research suggests that your gender identity can affect how dissociative symptoms show up, and if you identify with a diverse gender, you might encounter unique hurdles when it comes to integrating your identity. In therapy, acknowledging and honoring different identities, experiences, and cultural backgrounds is crucial. To provide effective care, the therapist needs to be sensitive to the specific obstacles faced by transgender individuals dealing with DID and adjust their therapeutic methods accordingly. This underscores the significance of acknowledging and respecting the range of identities within the realm of DID treatment.

Can trauma-informed care benefit individuals with DID even if they don't have a trauma history?

Trauma-informed care proves essential for individuals with DID, regardless of a formally documented trauma history. This method establishes a secure and encouraging setting, recognizing the potential effects of trauma and actively steering clear of retraumatization. Even in cases where a detailed trauma history remains uncertain or undisclosed, trauma-informed care cultivates a therapeutic alliance grounded in trust and sensitivity. It acknowledges that individuals might have undergone distressing events that they may not readily remember or share. By incorporating trauma-informed principles into therapeutic approaches, practitioners establish an environment conducive to both healing and personal development, irrespective of whether explicit details of a trauma history are revealed.

CONCLUSION

In understanding dissociative disorders and exploring the connection between dissociation and trauma, this book serves as a beacon of guidance. It goes beyond simply unraveling the dissociative disorders, providing us with accessible coping strategies and tools for recovery. At its core, this book discusses the critical link between dissociation and trauma. It emphasizes the ways in which the mind copes with overwhelming experiences, creating a distance from reality as a protective mechanism. By unraveling this connection, we gain a significant understanding of the roots of dissociative disorders, which paves the way for effective intervention and support.

This book emphasizes that diagnosing dissociative disorders requires a meticulous approach that combines thorough examinations, symptom discussions, and medical history reviews. The integration of specific tests, notably blood tests, serves to rule out potential physical factors influencing dissociative symptoms. This holistic diagnostic process ensures a nuanced understanding of an individual's well-being by considering both mental and physical health factors.

Our exploration extended to the array of treatment options available for dissociative disorders. From the development of personal crisis plans to practical strategies and relaxation techniques, the book provides a toolkit for navigating the challenges that dissociation can pose. Building a robust support system, a key element in the journey towards recovery, is highlighted as a crucial pillar in the treatment process.

As we wrap up this exploration, the key takeaway is crystal clear: Understanding is the first step towards healing. Recognizing the manifestations of dissociative disorders, comprehending their roots in trauma, and acknowledging the need for a multifaceted approach to treatment are the cornerstones of this guide. It is a holistic journey, encompassing not just the individual, but also the creation of a robust support system.

Dissociative disorders are often shrouded in stigma and misunderstanding. This book challenges that narrative by shedding light on the reality of these conditions. It encourages us to extend empathy, not only to ourselves, but also to others who may be struggling with similar challenges.

Therefore, it is important for **you** to engage in open conversations, challenge stigma, and champion mental health awareness. As you engage in conversations and disseminate the insights gained, you transform into a crucial advocate. Your role goes beyond personal growth; it involves creating a nurturing space for individuals facing mental health challenges. By sharing the wisdom acquired, you contribute to dismantling barriers, fostering empathy, and encouraging a supportive atmosphere. In doing so, you play a vital part in building a community that values and prioritizes mental well-being, paving the way for understanding, compassion, and positive change.

I extend my heartfelt wishes on your journey. May the insights gathered here be a guiding light as you navigate the complexities of dissociative disorders. Remember, you are not alone, and your journey towards healing is valid and significant.

Before we part ways, I invite you to share your thoughts on this book. Your feedback is invaluable, contributing to the ongoing dialogue surrounding dissociative disorders and mental health. Whether you found solace, discovered new perspectives, or have suggestions for improvement, your review can make a difference in someone else's journey.

In closing, let this book be a source of empowerment and enlightenment. May it serve as a bridge between understanding and action, fostering a community that embraces the complexities of mental health with compassion and knowledge. Thank you for joining me on this exploration, and I wish you strength, resilience, and healing on your path forward.

REFERENCES

ABS. (2022, June 19). *Dissociation vs. relaxation.* A Beautiful Soul Holistic Counseling. https://beautifulsoulcounseling.com/dissociation-vs-relaxation/

American Psychiatric Association. (2018). *Warning signs of mental illness.* Psychiatry. https://www.psychiatry.org/patients-families/warning-signs-of-mental-illness

Arkhipov, V. (1999). Memory dissociation: The approach to the study of retrieval processes. *Behavioural Brain Research, 106*(1-2), 39–46. https://doi.org/10.1016/s0166-4328(99)00090-x

Bailey, A. (2022a, January 7). *How to treat dissociative disorder.* Verywell Health. https://www.verywellhealth.com/how-to-treat-dissociative-disorder-5211865

Bailey, A. (2022b, January 7). *What causes switching with dissociative identity disorder?* Verywell Health. https://www.verywellhealth.com/dissociative-identity-disorder-switching-5212103

Berman, R. (2020, October 15). *How disassociation occurs in the brain.* Medical News Today.com. https://www.medicalnewstoday.com/articles/how-disassociation-occurs-in-the-brain

Birt, J. (2022, December 22). *Building good relationships at work: How to do it and why they're important.* Indeed Career Guide. https://www.indeed.com/career-advice/career-development/building-relationships

Boyer, S. M., Caplan, J. E., & Edwards, L. K. (2022). Trauma-related dissociation and the dissociative disorders. *Delaware Journal of Public Health, 8*(2), 78–84. https://doi.org/10.32481/djph.2022.05.010

Braun, W. (1947). Bacterial dissociation. *Bacteriological Reviews, 11*(2), 75–114. https://doi.org/10.1128/mmbr.11.2.75-114.1947

Brennan, D. (2021, October 25). *Psychological Benefits of Routines.* WebMD. https://www.webmd.com/mental-health/psychological-benefits-of-routine

Broady, K. (2019, October 8). *Our new DID community forum is OPEN!* Discussing Dissociation. https://www.discussingdissociation.com/2019/10/our-new-did-community-forum-is-open/

Carlson, E., & Putnam, F. (n.d.). *Dissociative experiences scale-II (DES-II).* https://emdrtherapyvolusia.com/wp-content/uploads/2016/12/DES_II.pdf

Causes. (n.d.). Mind. https://www.mind.org.uk/information-support/types-of-mental-health-problems/dissociation-and-dissociative-disorders/causes/

Center, B. A. C. (2023, August 4). *CBT for derealization: Understanding causes, symp-*

toms, and treatment*. Bay Area CBT Center. https://bayareacbtcenter.com/cbt-for-derealization-dissociation/

Cervantes, J. (2020, January 22). *How is time management important for your mental health?* Painted Brain. https://paintedbrain.org/blog/how-is-time-management-important-for-your-mental-health

Cherry, K. (2021, May 20). *What Is self-monitoring?* Verywell Mind. https://www.verywellmind.com/what-is-self-monitoring-5179838

Cikanavicius , D. (2019, March 10). *How childhood trauma and dissociation result in horrible adulthood problems*. Psych Central. https://psychcentral.com/blog/psychology-self/2019/03/trauma-dissociation-problems

Cintron, G., Salloum, A., Blair-Andrews, Z., & Storch, E. A. (2017). Parents' descriptions of young children's dissociative reactions after trauma. *Journal of Trauma & Dissociation, 19*(5), 500–513. https://doi.org/10.1080/15299732.2017.1387886

Cleveland Clinic. (2021, May 25). *Dissociative Identity Disorder (Multiple Personality Disorder)*. Cleveland Clinic; Cleveland Clinic. https://my.clevelandclinic.org/health/diseases/9792-dissociative-identity-disorder-multiple-personality-disorder

Cleveland Clinic. (2023). *Dissociative disorders: Types, causes, symptoms & treatment*. Cleveland Clinic. https://my.clevelandclinic.org/health/diseases/17749-dissociative-disorders

Costa, R. M. (2020). Dissociation (defense mechanism). *Encyclopedia of Personality and Individual Differences*, 1165–1167. https://doi.org/10.1007/978-3-319-24612-3_1375

Creating healthy routines. (n.d.). https://mhanational.org/sites/default/files/Handout%20-%20Creating%20Healthy%20Routines.pdf

Defeating complex trauma with self-compassion. (2022, July 8). Learn about DID. https://www.learnaboutdid.com/2022/07/08/defeating-complex-trauma-with-self-compassion/

Dimochkino. (2022, January 28). *What Is self-monitoring? Meaning, examples & checklist [2022]*. HIGH5 TEST. https://high5test.com/self-monitoring/

Dissociative identity disorder: What you need to know. (2022, August 29). McLean Hospital. https://www.mcleanhospital.org/essential/did

Dissociation. (2020). Tstresources.org. https://www.tstresources.org/dissociation/

Dissociation and dissociative disorders. (2023, February 17). Vic. https://www.betterhealth.vic.gov.au/health/conditionsandtreatments/dissociation-and-dissociative-disorders

Dissociation anxiety: Symptoms, treatments, and facts. (2021, June 16). *Southern California* Sunrise Recovery Mental Health Treatment. https://socalsunrisemh.com/dissociation-anxiety-symptoms-treatments-facts/

Dissociative experiences scale. (2023, December 22). Wikipedia. https://en.wikipedia. org/wiki/Dissociative_Experiences_Scale

Do you manage your time well?. (2022, April 23). McLean Hospital. https://www. mcleanhospital.org/essential/do-you-manage-your-time-well

Drescher, J. (2022, October). *What are dissociative disorders?* American Psychiatric Association.   https://www.psychiatry.org/patients-families/dissociative-disor ders/what-are-dissociative-disorders

Dutra, L., Bureau, J.-F., Holmes, B., Lyubchik, A., & Lyons-Ruth, K. (2009). Quality of early care and childhood trauma. *The Journal of Nervous and Mental Disease, 197*(6), 383–390. https://doi.org/10.1097/nmd.0b013e3181a653b7

Eddins, R. (2020, April 1). *Grounding techniques & self soothing for emotional regula- tion.* Eddins Counseling Group. https://eddinscounseling.com/grounding-tech niques-self-soothing-emotional-regulation/

Effa, C. (2023, February 27). *Schizophrenia vs. dissociative identity disorder.* Medical News Today. https://www.medicalnewstoday.com/articles/dissociative-iden tity-disorder-and-schizophrenia

18 grounding techniques to help relieve anxiety. (n.d.). Calm Blog. Retrieved February 9, 2024, from https://www.calm.com/blog/grounding-techniques

Elmer, J. (2021, April 12). *Dissociative Identity Disorder (DID) vs. schizophrenia: What's the difference?* Psych Central. https://psychcentral.com/schizophrenia/did-vs- schizophrenia

Famous people with dissociative identity disorder. (2015, April 6). HRF. https:// healthresearchfunding.org/famous-people-dissociative-identity-disorder/

Ferguson, S. (2023, April 3). *How common is DID? Early symptoms, causes.* Healthline. https://www.healthline.com/health/how-common-is-did

5, 4, 3, 2, 1 — a simple grounding exercise to calm anxiety. (2023, September 12). Calm Blog.   https://www.calm.com/blog/5-4-3-2-1-a-simple-exercise-to-calm-the- mind

Five ways to build strong relationships. (n.d.). My World of Work. https://careers. myworldofwork.co.uk/career-advice/growing-and-using-your-network/five- ways-to-build-strong-relationships

For friends and family. (n.d.). Mind. https://www.mind.org.uk/information- support/types-of-mental-health-problems/dissociation-and-dissociative-disor ders/for-friends-and-family/

Freifeld, L. (2013, March 21). *8 tips for developing positive relationships.* Training. https://trainingmag.com/8-tips-for-developing-positive-relationships/

Future Self Visualization: 10 best practices and 11 advantages. (2017, July 14). https:// smartleadershiphut.com/visualization/future-self-visualization/

Giuams. (2018, December 28). *My strange experience with dissociative amnesia.* https://www.reddit.com/r/Glitch_in_the_Matrix/comments/aa5iw0/my_s

trange_experience_with_dissociative_amnesia/?utm_source=share&
utm_medium=web3x&utm_name=web3xcss&utm_term=1&utm_content=
share_button

Grounding 101: Featuring 101 grounding techniques! (2016, December 23). Beauty after Bruises. https://www.beautyafterbruises.org/blog/grounding101

Grounding techniques. (n.d.). Psychology Tools. https://www.psychologytools.com/resource/grounding-techniques/

Guérin-Marion, C., Sezlik, S., & Bureau, J.-F. (2020). Developmental and attachment-based perspectives on dissociation: beyond the effects of maltreatment. *European Journal of Psychotraumatology, 11*(1), 1802908. https://doi.org/10.1080/20008198.2020.1802908

Harnessing hope: Practical tips for managing dissociation. (2023, January 11). Human Integrated Performance. https://blog.yeghip.com/harnessing-hope-practical-tips-for-managing-dissociation

Harris, R. (n.d.). *Some Powerful Practic Al tips.* Retrieved February 9, 2024, from https://www.actmindfully.com.au/upimages/Working_With_Dissociation_-_Russ_Harris_-_www.ImLearningACT.com.pdf

Haycock, D. (2010, October 25). *Probing question: How do schizophrenia and DID differ?* Penn State University. https://www.psu.edu/news/research/story/probing-question-how-do-schizophrenia-and-did-differ/

Helping a loved one who dissociates. (2015, May 2). Dr Catherine Hynes. https://catherinehynes.net/helping-a-loved-one-with-therapy/loved-one-who-dissociates/

How childhood trauma and dissociation result in horrible adulthood problems. (2019, March 10). Psych Central. https://psychcentral.com/blog/psychology-self/2019/03/trauma-dissociation-problems

How to stay calm when emotions overwhelm you: 10 grounding techniques. (2019, January 10). Hush Your Mind. https://www.hushyourmind.com/how-to-stay-calm-10-grounding-techniques/

Huggins, P. (n.d.). *#1 Free meditation app for sleep, relax & more.* Insight Timer. Retrieved February 9, 2024, from https://insighttimer.com/paulahuggins/guided-meditations/safe-space-visualisation

Information from your patient aligned care team visualization/guided imagery. (n.d.). https://www.mirecc.va.gov/cih-visn2/Documents/Patient_Education_Handouts/Visualization_Guided_Imagery_2013.pdf

Jans, T., Schneck-Seif, S., Weigand, T., Schneider, W., Ellgring, H., Wewetzer, C., & Warnke, A. (2008). Long-term outcome and prognosis of dissociative disorder with onset in childhood or adolescence. *Child and Adolescent Psychiatry and Mental Health, 2*(1). https://doi.org/10.1186/1753-2000-2-19

Kennerley, H. (1996). Cognitive therapy of dissociative symptoms associated with trauma. *British Journal of Clinical Psychology, 35*(3), 325–340. https://doi.org/10.1111/j.2044-8260.1996.tb01188.x

Krause-Utz, A., Frost, R., Winter, D., & Elzinga, B. M. (2019). Dissociation and alterations in brain function and structure: Implications for borderline personality disorder. *Current Psychiatry Reports, 19*(1). https://doi.org/10.1007/s11920-017-0757-y

Matthew Tull. (2019). *The Double-edged sword of childhood trauma and dissociation.* Verywell Mind. https://www.verywellmind.com/how-trauma-can-lead-to-dissociative-disorders-2797534

Mayo Clinic Staff. (2017). *Dissociative disorders: Diagnosis and treatment.* Mayo Clinic. https://www.mayoclinic.org/diseases-conditions/dissociative-disorders/diagnosis-treatment/drc-20355221

Mayo Clinic Staff. (2017, November 17). *Dissociative disorders: Symptoms and causes.* Mayo Clinic. https://www.mayoclinic.org/diseases-conditions/dissociative-disorders/symptoms-causes/syc-20355215

Mental health crisis plan. (2021, August 20). Psych Central. https://psychcentral.com/health/creating-a-mental-health-crisis-plan#whats-a-crisis-plan

Mental health crisis plan: What is it, importance and types. (n.d.). Mind 24-7. Retrieved February 9, 2024, from https://www.mind24-7.com/blog/the-importance-of-creating-a-mental-health-crisis-plan/

Mental illness. (2019). Healthdirect Australia. https://www.healthdirect.gov.au/mental-illness

Mental illness and the family: Recognizing warning signs and how to cope. (2019). Mental Health America. https://www.mhanational.org/recognizing-warning-signs

Mind. (2019, March). *About dissociation.* Mind. https://www.mind.org.uk/information-support/types-of-mental-health-problems/dissociation-and-dissociative-disorders/about-dissociation/

My support forums: Dissociative disorders. (n.d.). My Support Forums. Retrieved February 9, 2024, from https://mysupportforums.org/dissociative-disorders/

NAMI. (2020). *Dissociative disorders | NAMI: National Alliance on Mental Illness.* NAMI. https://www.nami.org/About-Mental-Illness/Mental-Health-Conditions/Dissociative-Disorders

News, N. (2022, November 3). *Study sheds new light on brain activity related to dissociative symptoms.* Neuroscience News. https://neurosciencenews.com/dissociation-brain-21780/

NHS. (2020, August 10). *Dissociative disorders.* NHS. https://www.nhs.uk/mental-health/conditions/dissociative-disorders/

Nijenhuis, E. R. S. (2001). Somatoform dissociation. *Journal of Trauma & Dissociation, 1*(4), 7–32. https://doi.org/10.1300/j229v01n04_02

Northwestern Medicine Staff. (2016, August 15). *Health benefits of having a routine.* Northwestern Medicine; Northwestern Medicine. https://www.nm.org/health beat/healthy-tips/health-benefits-of-having-a-routine

Nowak, L. (2019, June 19). *How dissociative identity disorder affects daily life and how you can help.* BrightQuest Treatment Centers. https://www.brightquest.com/ blog/how-dissociative-identity-disorder-affects-daily-life-and-how-you-can-help/

Omar. (2023, April 28). *Someone I love is experiencing dissociation: How can I help?* Alter Behavioral Health. https://alterbehavioralhealth.com/blog/someone-i-love-is-experiencing-dissociation-how-can-i-help/

Ozdemir, O., Guzel Ozdemir, P., Boysan, M., & Yilmaz, E. (2015). The Relationships between dissociation, attention, and memory dysfunction. *Noro Psikiyatri Arsivi, 52*(1), 36–41. https://doi.org/10.5152/npa.2015.7390

Patel, H., & Pharm, M. (2018, May 23). *Dissociative identity disorder causes.* News-Medical. https://www.news-medical.net/health/Dissociative-Identity-Disorder-Causes.aspx

Psychosis and dissociative disorders. (2017, January 13). Active Living Alliance for Canadians with a Disability. https://ala.ca/resource/tip-sheets/psychosis-and-dissociative-disorders

Putnam, F. W. (1991). Dissociative disorders in children and adolescents. A developmental perspective. *The Psychiatric Clinics of North America, 14*(3), 519–531. https://pubmed.ncbi.nlm.nih.gov/1946022/

Putnam, F. W. (1996). Child development and dissociation. *Child and adolescent psychiatric clinics of North America, 5*(2), 285–302. https://doi.org/10.1016/s1056-4993(18)30367-5

Raison, A., & Andrea, S. (2023). Childhood trauma in patients with dissociative identity disorder: A systematic review of data from 1990 to 2022. *European Journal of Trauma & Dissociation, 7*(1), 100310. https://doi.org/10.1016/j.ejtd.2022.100310

Raypole, C. (2019, May 24). *30 grounding techniques to quiet distressing thoughts.* Healthline. https://www.healthline.com/health/grounding-techniques

Dive into anything. (n.d.). Reddit. Retrieved February 9, 2024, from https://www.reddit.com/r/DID/wiki/faq/#wiki_1._i_don.27t_remember_any_trauma._does_that_mean_i_don.27t_have_did.3F

Rege, S. (2023, January 20). *The neuroscience of dissociation: Clinical application in trauma disorders.* Psych Scene Hub. https://psychscenehub.com/psychinsights/the-neuroscience-of-dissociation

Regional online communities. (n.d.). ISSTD. Retrieved February 9, 2024, from https://www.isst-d.org/join-isstd/regional-online-communities/

Rufer, M., Held, D., Cremer, J., Fricke, S., Moritz, S., Peter, H., & Hand, I. (2005).

Dissociation as a predictor of cognitive behavior therapy outcome in patients with obsessive—compulsive disorder. *Psychotherapy and Psychosomatics, 75*(1), 40–46. https://doi.org/10.1159/000089225

Sajjadi, S. F., Sellbom, M., Gross, J., & Hayne, H. (2021). Dissociation and false memory: The moderating role of trauma and cognitive ability. *Memory, 29*(9), 1–15. https://doi.org/10.1080/09658211.2021.1963778

Sar, V. (2016). Formation and functions of alter personalities in dissociative ddentity Disorder: A theoretical and clinical elaboration. *Journal of Psychology & Clinical Psychiatry, 6*(6). https://doi.org/10.15406/jpcpy.2016.06.00385

Self-compassion. (n.d.). Trauma informed. https://trauma-informed.ca/recovery/phases-of-trauma-recovery/self-compassion/

Self-compassion: What it is and how to get better at it. (n.d.). Everyday Health. https://www.everydayhealth.com/emotional-health/tips-for-showing-yourself-some-self-compassion/

Socratic questions. (n.d.). https://www.therapistaid.com/worksheets/socratic-questioning

Subramanyam, A., Somaiya, M., Shankar, S., Nasirabadi, M., Shah, H., Paul, I., & Ghildiyal, R. (2020). Psychological interventions for dissociative disorders. *Indian Journal of Psychiatry, 62*(8), 280. https://doi.org/10.4103/psychiatry.indianjpsychiatry_777_19

Swaim , E. (2022, November 7). *Why dissociation happens and how to handle it.* Healthline. https://www.healthline.com/health/mental-health/dissociative-defense-mechanism

Tartakovsky, M., & read, M. S. L. updated: 14 J. 2020~ 9 min. (2017, December 17). *Dissociative identity disorder treatment.* Psych Central. https://psychcentral.com/disorders/dissociative-identity-disorder/treatment

Team, T. G. (2017, December 29). *Best of 2017: GoodTherapy.org's Top Resources for Dissociation.* Good Therapy Blog. https://www.goodtherapy.org/blog/best-dissociation-websites-2017-1229174/

10 Grounding Techniques for Dissociation. (n.d.). Sarai Monk Psychotherapy. Retrieved February 9, 2024, from https://www.saraimonk.com/blog/10-grounding-techniques-for-dissociation

The body as a shared whole: Using visualization techniques to treat dissociation. (n.d.). Catalog. Retrieved February 9, 2024, from https://catalog.psychotherapynetworker.org/item/the-body-shared-wholeusing-visualization-techniques-treat-dissociation-69024

The secret and life-changing impact of early childhood abuse: Dissociative identity disorder. (n.d.). McLean Hospital. https://www.mcleanhospital.org/essential/early-childhood-abuse-dissociative-identity-disorder

Therapist, M. G. Q., Licensed Marriage and Family. (2022, February 21).

Grounding techniques to help you deal with dissociation. Michael G. Quirke, MFT. https://michaelgquirke.com/grounding-techniques-to-help-you-deal-with-dissociation/

Top tips on building and maintaining healthy relationships. (2023). Mental Health Foundation. https://www.mentalhealth.org.uk/our-work/public-engagement/healthy-relationships/top-tips-building-and-maintaining-healthy-relationships

Trauma and resilience for adults. (n.d.). Greater Good in Education. https://ggie.berkeley.edu/my-well-being/trauma-and-resilience-for-adults/

Trauma during adulthood. (2022, December 29). Samhsa. https://www.samhsa.gov/resource/dbhis/trauma-during-adulthood

Treatment for dissociative disorders. (n.d.). The Recovery Village Drug and Alcohol Rehab. https://www.therecoveryvillage.com/mental-health/dissociative-disorders/treatment/

Understanding dissociative disorders understanding dissociative disorders. (n.d.). Retrieved February 9, 2024, from https://www.slamrecoverycollege.co.uk/uploads/2/6/5/2/26525995/dissociative_disorders.pdf

van Minnen, A., & Tibben, M. (2021). A brief cognitive-behavioural treatment approach for PTSD and dissociative identity disorder, a case report. *Journal of Behavior Therapy and Experimental Psychiatry, 72*(101655), 101655. https://doi.org/10.1016/j.jbtep.2021.101655

Vancappel, A., & El-Hage, W. (2023). A cognitive behavioral model for dissociation: Conceptualization, empirical evidence and clinical implications. *Journal of Behavioral and Cognitive Therapy.* https://doi.org/10.1016/j.jbct.2023.05.003

Washington, N. (2023, February 13). *DID vs. schizophrenia: What's the difference?* Healthline. https://www.healthline.com/health/schizophrenia/did-vs-schizophrenia

West, M. (2022, April 21). *Guided imagery: Techniques, benefits, and more.* Www.medicalnewstoday.com. https://www.medicalnewstoday.com/articles/guided-imagery

What are the benefits of self-monitoring your emotions and stress levels at work? (n.d.). Www.linkedin.com. https://www.linkedin.com/advice/0/what-benefits-self-monitoring-your-emotions-stress

What self-care can I do when I'm dissociating? (2023, January). Mind. https://www.mind.org.uk/information-support/types-of-mental-health-problems/dissociation-and-dissociative-disorders/coping-with-dissociation/

What treatments are there for dissociative disorders? (2023, January). Mind. https://www.mind.org.uk/information-support/types-of-mental-health-problems/dissociation-and-dissociative-disorders/treatments-for-dissociative-disorders/